£11.80

Elster's Folly
by Ellen Wood

Copyright © 2019 by HardPress

Address:
HardPress
8345 NW 66TH ST #2561
MIAMI FL 33166-2626
USA
Email: info@hardpress.net

600071779.

ELSTER'S FOLLY.

LONDON:
ROBSON AND SON, GREAT NORTHERN PRINTING WORKS,
PANCRAS ROAD, N.W.

ELSTER'S FOLLY.

A Novel.

BY

MRS. HENRY WOOD,

AUTHOR OF "EAST LYNNE," "ST. MARTIN'S EVE," ETC. ETC.

IN THREE VOLUMES.

VOL. I.

SECOND EDITION.

LONDON:
TINSLEY BROTHERS, 18 CATHERINE ST. STRAND.
1866.

[All rights of translation and reproduction reserved.]

CONTENTS OF VOL. I.

CHAP.		PAGE
I.	BY THE EARLY TRAIN	1
II.	WILLY GUM	31
III.	ANNE ASHTON	53
IV.	THE COUNTESS DOWAGER	78
V.	A RISING JEALOUSY	100
VI.	AN ENCOUNTER AT THE BRIDGE	125
VII.	CLERK GUM'S SHUTTERS	153
VIII.	THE WAGER BOATS	173
IX.	WAITING FOR DINNER	201
X.	MR. PIKE'S VISIT	225
XI.	THE INQUEST	245
XII.	MR. PIKE'S WHISPER TO JABEZ GUM	265
XIII.	PITCH-POTS BURNING	289

ELSTER'S FOLLY.

CHAPTER I.

BY THE EARLY TRAIN.

THE slanting beams of the ascending sun threw their light abroad on a glorious August morning, and the little world below began to awaken into life—the life of another day of sanguine pleasure or of fretting care. Not on many fairer scenes did those beams shed their radiance than on one that might be seen almost in the heart of England; but nearly all landscapes look beautiful in the early light of a summer's morning. The county, one of the midland—or it may be more correct to say a south-midland — was justly celebrated for its charming scenery; its rich woods, its smiling plains, its river, and its gentle streams. The harvest was nearly gathered—this had been a late season—but a few fields of golden grain, in process of reaping, imparted their warm tints to the landscape. In no part of the county had the beauties of nature been bestowed with a more lavish hand than on this, the village of Calne, situate about seven miles from the county town. It was an aristocratic village, on the whole: the beautiful seat of the Earl of Hartledon, rising close to it, had caused a few good families to settle there, and the nest of white villas gave to the place a well-to-do, picturesque appearance. But it contained the full proportion of the poor or labouring class; and these people were getting very much into the habit of writing the village (when they had occasion to write it), in accordance with its pronunciation—Cawn. Phonetic spelling was more in their line than Walker's Dictionary. Of what may be called the middle class there were few, if any, in the village: there were the gentry, the small shopkeepers, and the poor.

Calne had recently been exalted into importance. A year or two previous to this bright August morning, some good genius had brought a railway to it—a railway and a station, and all its accompanying work and bustle. A great many trains passed it in the day; for it was in the direct line of route from the county town, Garchester, to London, and the traffic was increasing. People wondered what travellers had done, and what sort of a round they had to traverse, before this direct line was made.

The village itself lay rather in a hollow, but the ground rose to a gentle eminence on either side. On the one eminence, that to the west, was situated the station; on the other eminence, towards the east, rose the peer's large, fine, stone mansion, Hartledon House. The railway took a slight detour on the outside of Calne, and was a conspicuous feature to any who chose to look at it; for its supporting ground had been raised above the hollow of the village, to correspond with the height at either end.

Six o'clock was close at hand, and the station began to show some symptoms of existence. The station-master came out of his cottage near, and opened one or two doors on the platform. He had held the office hardly a year yet; and had come to Calne a stranger. He sat down in his little bureau of a place, on the door of which was written " Station-master—Private," and began sorting some papers on the high desk before him. A few minutes, and the clock struck six; upon which he went out on the platform. It was an open station, as these small stations generally are, the scant waiting-rooms and offices on either side scarcely at all obstructing the view of the country, and the master looked far out in the distance; towards the east, beyond the low-lying houses of the village, shading his eyes with his hand from the dazzling sun.

" Her's late this morning."

The interruption came from the surly porter, who was standing by. He alluded to the expected train, which ought to have been in some minutes before. According to the precise time, as laid down in the way-bills, it should reach Calne seven minutes before six.

"They have a heavy load, perhaps," remarked the station-master.

The train was one chiefly for goods—a slow train, taking goodness knows how many hours to travel from London. It would bring passengers also; but few availed themselves of it. Now and then it happened that the station at Calne was opened for nothing, and the train just slackened its speed and went on, leaving no goods or any thing else behind it. Sometimes it took a few early travellers from Calne to Garchester, especially on Wednesdays and Saturdays, Garchester market-days; but it rarely left passengers at Calne.

"Did you hear the news, Mr. Markham?" asked the porter.

"What news?" returned the master.

"I heered it last night. Jim come into the Elster Arms and said it, and *he'd* heered it at Garchester. We are going to have two more sets o' telegraph wires here; I wonder how much more work they'll think of giving us to do?"

"So you were at the Elster Arms again last night, Jones?" remarked the master, his tone implying reproof, while he passed over in silence Mr. Jones's item of news.

"I warn't in for above an hour," grumbled the man.

"Well, it is your own look-out, Jones: I have said what I could to you at odd times; but I believe it has only tried your patience; so I'll say no more."

"Has my wife been here again complaining?" asked the man, raising his face in fierce anger.

"No; I have not seen your wife, except at church, for these two months. But I know what public-houses are to you, and I was thinking of your little children."

"Ugh!" growled the man, not gratified apparently at the reminder of his flock, "there's a peck o' *them!* Here her comes!"

The last sentence was spoken in a different tone; one of relieved alacrity, either at the getting rid of the subject, or the coming up of the train. It was about opposite to Hartledon when he caught sight of it, and it came on swiftly, with a shrill whistle, skirting the village it towered above; a long line of covered waggons with a passenger carriage or two attached. Slackening its pace gradually, but not in time, it shot past the station, and had to back into it again, and stop.

The guard came out of his box and opened the door of one of the carriages—a dirty-looking second-class one; the other was a third-class; and a gentleman leaped out. A tall, slender man, of about four-and-twenty; a man of evidently good birth and breeding. He wore a light summer over-coat on his well-cut clothes, and had a most attractive face.

"Is there any law against your putting on a first-class carriage to this night train?" he asked the guard, in a pleasing voice.

"Well, sir, we never get first-class passengers by it," replied the man, "or hardly any passengers at all, for the matter of that. We are too long on the road for passengers to come by us."

"It might happen, though," returned the gentleman, significantly. "At any rate, I suppose there's no law against your carriages being clean, whatever their class. Look at that one."

He pointed to the one he had just come from, as he walked up to the station-master. The guard looked cross, and gave the carriage-door a bang.

"Was a portmanteau left here last night by the last train from London?" inquired the traveller of the station-master.

"No, sir; nothing was left here. At least I think not. Any name on it, sir?"

"Elster."

A quick glance from the station-master's eyes greeted the answer. Elster was the name of the family at Hartledon. He wondered whether this could be one of them, or whether the name was but a passing coincidence.

"There was no portmanteau left, was there, Jones?" asked the master.

"There couldn't have been," returned the porter, who was perpetually touching his hat to the stranger. "I wasn't on last night; Jim was; but it would have been put in the office for sure; and there's not a ghost of a thing in it this morning."

"It must have been taken on to Garchester," remarked the traveller; and, turning to the guard, he gave him directions to look after it, and despatch it back again by the first train, slipping at the same time a gratuity into his hand.

The guard touched his hat humbly; he now knew who the gentleman was. And he went into inward repentance for the banging of the carriage-door, as he got into his box, and the engine and train puffed on.

"You'll send it up as soon as it comes," said the traveller to the station-master.

"Where to, sir?"

The stranger raised his eyes in slight surprise, and pointed to the great house in the distance. He had assumed that he was known.

"To Hartledon."

Then he *was* one of the family! The station-master touched his hat. Mr. Jones, in the background, touched his, and for the first time the gentleman's eye fell upon him, as he was turning to leave the platform.

"Why, Jones! It's never you?"

"Yes it is, sir." But Mr. Jones looked abashed as he acknowledged himself; and it may be observed that his language, when addressing this gentleman, was a slight improvement upon the homely phraseology of his every-day life.

"But—you are surely not working here!—a porter!"

"My business fell through, sir," returned the man. "I'm here till I can turn myself round, sir, and get into it again."

"What caused it to fall through?" asked the traveller; a kindly sympathy in his fine blue eyes.

Mr. Jones shuffled upon one foot. He would not have given the true answer for the world: "drinking."

"There's such opposition started up in the place, sir; folks 'ud draw your heart's blood from you if they could. And then I've got such a lot of mouths to feed. I can't think what the plague such a tribe of children comes for. Nobody wants 'em."

The gentleman laughed; but he put no further questions. Remembering somewhat of Mr. Jones's propensity to errant habits in the old days, he thought perhaps something besides children and opposition had had to do with the downfall. He stood a moment looking at the station, which had not been completed when he last saw it—and a very pretty station it was, surrounded by its parterres of gay-coloured flowers—and then went down the road.

"I suppose he's one of the Hartledon family, Jones?" said the station-master, looking after him.

"He's the Earl's brother," replied Mr. Jones, relapsing into sulkiness again. "There be but them two left; t'other died. Wonder if they be coming to Hartledon again? Calne haven't seemed the same since they quitted it."

"Which is this one?"

"He can't be any body but himself," retorted Mr. Jones, irascibly, deeming the question a superfluous one. "There be but the two left, I say,—the Earl and him; every body knows him for the Honourable Percival Elster. T'other son, George, died; leastways was murdered."

"Murdered!" echoed the station-master, aghast.

"I don't see as it could be called much else but murder," was Mr. Jones's answer. "He went out with my lord's gamekeepers one night and got shot in a poaching fray. 'Twas never known for certain who fired the shot, but I think I could put my finger on the man if I tried. Much good *that* 'ud be of, though! There's no proof."

"What is it that you are saying, Jones?" cried the station-master, staring at his subordinate, and perhaps wondering whether he had already that morning paid a visit to the tap of the Elster Arms.

"I'm saying nothing that half the place didn't say at the time, Mr. Markham. *You* hadn't come here then. Mr. Elster—he was the Honourable George—went out one night with the keepers, when warm work was expected, and he got shot for his pains. He lived some weeks, but they couldn't cure him. It was in the late lord's time; *he* died soon after, and the place have been deserted ever since."

"And who do you suppose fired the shot?"

"Don't know that it 'ud be safe to say," rejoined the man. "He might give my neck a twist some dark night if he heerd on't. He's the blackest sheep we've got in Calne, sir."

"I suppose you mean Pike," said the master. "He has the character for being that, I believe. I've seen no harm in the man myself."

"Well, it was Pike," said the porter; "that is, it was him that some of us suspected; and that's how Mr. George Elster came by his death; and this one, Mr. Percival, shot up into notice, as being the only one left, except Lord Elster."

"And who's Lord Elster?" asked the station-master, not remembering to have heard the title before.

Mr. Jones received the question with proper contempt. Having been familiar with Hartledon and its inmates all his life, he had as little compassion for those not so, as he would have had for a man who did not understand that Garchester was in England.

"The present Earl of Hartledon," said he shortly. "In his father's lifetime—and the old lord lived to see Mr. George buried—he was Lord Elster. There ain't one of my tribe of brats but could tell that any Lord Elster must be the eldest son of the Earl of Hartledon," he concluded, with a fling at his superior.

"Ah, well, I have had other things to do since I came here, apart from inquiring into titles and folks that don't concern me," remarked the master. "What a good-looking man he is!"

The praise applied to Mr. Elster, after whom he was throwing a parting look. Jones gave an ungracious grunt of assent, and turned into the shed where the lamps were kept, to begin his morning's work.

All the world would have been ready to echo the station-master's words as to the good looks of Percival Elster, known universally amidst his friends as Val; for these good looks did not lie so much in actual beauty—which one lauds, and another carps at, according to its style—as in the exceedingly pleasant expression of countenance; a gift that finds its weight with all. He had a bright face, his complexion was fair and fresh, his eyes were blue and smiling, his features were good; and as he walked down the road, and lifted his hat momentarily to push his light hair— as much of a gold colour as hair ever is—from his brow, and gave the "good-day" cordially and brightly to as many as met him on their way to work,—few strangers but would have given to him a second look of admiration. A physiognomist might have found fault with the face; and, while admitting its sweet expression, would have condemned it for its utter want of resolution. Want of that, the inability to say "no" to any sort of persuasion, whether for good or for ill; in short, a total absence of what may be called moral courage, had been from his childhood Val Elster's besetting sin. There was a joke against little Val when he was a boy of seven. Some playmates had insisted upon his walking into a pond, and standing there. Poor Val, completely unable to say "no," walked in, and was nearly drowned for his pains. It had been made a joke against him then; how many such "jokes" could have been brought against him since he grew up, Val himself could alone tell. As the child had been, so was the man; the scrapes that his irresolution brought him into he did not care to glance at; and while all too aware of his one lamentable deficiency, he was equally aware that he was powerless to make stand against it. People, in speaking of this, called it "Elster's Folly." The exceeding sensitiveness as to the feelings of other people, let them be his equals or his inferiors, was, in a degree, one of the causes of this yielding nature; and he would almost rather have died than offer any one a personal offence, an insulting word or look. There are such characters in the world: none can deny that they are amiable; but, O, how unfit to battle with life!

Mr. Elster walked slowly through the village, on his way to Hartledon, whose inmates he would presently take by surprise. It was about twenty months since he had been there. He had quitted Hartledon at the close of the last winter but one;

an appointment having been obtained for him abroad, as an *attaché* to the Paris embassy. Ten months of service, when some scrape he got into caused him (there was a good deal of private interest brought to bear) to be removed to Vienna; but he had not remained there very long. He seemed to have a propensity for getting into trouble, or rather an inability to keep out of it. Latterly he had been staying in London with his brother, the Earl.

His thoughts wandered to the past, as he looked at the chimneys of Hartledon—all he could see of it—from the hollow ground. He remembered the happy time when they had been children in it; five of them—the three boys and the two girls—he himself being the youngest and the pet. His eldest sister, Margaret, had been the first to go from it; she married Sir James Cooper, and went with him to his remote home in Scotland, where she was still. The second to go was Laura, who married Captain Level, and accompanied him to India. Then he, Val, a young man in his teens, went out into the world, and did all sorts of harm in it in an unintentional sort of way; for Percival Elster never did wrong by premeditation. Next came the death of his mother; he was called home from a sojourn in Scotland—where his stay had been prolonged from the result of an accident—to bid her farewell. Then he was at home for a year or more, making love to charming Anne Ashton. The next move was his departure for Paris; close upon which, within a fortnight, occurred the calamity to his brother George. He came back from Paris to see him in London, whither George had been conveyed for medical advice, and there seemed then a chance of his recovery; but it was not borne out, and the ill-fated young man died. The Earl's death was the next; he had an incurable complaint, and his death followed close upon his son's. Lord Elster became Earl of Hartledon; and he, Val, presumptive heir. Presumptive heir! Val Elster was heir to all sorts of follies, but—

"Good morning to your lordship!"

The speaker was a man in a smock-frock, passing with a reaping-hook on his shoulder. Mr.

Elster's sunny face and cheery voice gave back the salutation with tenfold heartiness, smiling at the " lordship." Half the peasantry had been used to address the brothers so, indiscriminately: they were all lords to them.

The interruption awoke Mr. Elster from his thoughts, and he marched gaily on down the middle of the road, noting the familiar features of the route. The shops—small shops, and most of them general ones, selling every thing—were on his right hand, the line of rail being behind them. The few white villas lay scattered on his left, and behind them, but not to be seen from this village street, wound the river, parallel, as may be said, with the railway; both parallel with the village that lay between them. Soon the houses ceased; it was but a small place at best; and, after an open space, came the church. It was on his right hand, on the same side as the passed shops, lying a little way back from the road, and surrounded by a large churchyard. Nearly opposite to it, on the other side the road, but lying very far back from it, was a handsome modern white house; its beautiful gardens sloping down nearly to the river behind. It was the residence of the rector, Dr. Ashton, a wealthy man and high church dignitary, prebendary and sub-dean of Garchester Cathedral. Percival Elster looked at it fondly, yearningly, if haply he might see the face of one he loved well; but the blinds were drawn before the windows, and the inmates were no doubt steeped in quiet repose.

"If she could but know I was here!" he fondly aspirated.

On again a few steps, and a slight turn in the road brought him to another house, a small redbrick dwelling, on the same side as the church, with green shutters to its lower windows. It lay back in the midst of a garden well stocked with vegetables, fruit, and with the more ordinary and brighter garden-flowers. A straight path led to the house-door—a well-kept door, its paint fresh and green, its brass-plate as bright as rubbing could make it. Mr. Elster could not read the writing on the plate from where he was, but he knew it by heart: "Jabez Gum, Parish Clerk."

And there was a smaller plate indicating other offices that Jabez Gum held.

"I wonder if Jabez is as shadowy as ever?" thought Mr. Elster, as he walked on.

One feature more, and that is the last you shall hear of until Hartledon's reached. Close to the clerk's garden, on a bit of waste land, stood a small wooden building, no better than a shed. It had once been a stable, but so long as Percival Hartledon could remember it, was nothing but a receptacle for schoolboys to hide in, when playing at hide-and-seek. Many a time had he hid there. Something different in this shed now struck his eye; the former doorway had been boarded up, and a long iron tube, looking like a thin chimney, ascended from its roof.

"Who on earth has been putting that to it?" exclaimed Mr. Elster.

A little way onwards, and he came to the lodge-gates of Hartledon, on the right: for the house was on the same side as the rectory, its park stretching out to the east, its grounds far more beautiful and extensive than those of the rectory, descending to the river. As he went in at the side-gate, which stood wide open — little attention being paid to these things in the absence of the family—he turned his head on the familiar road he had quitted, and most distinctly saw a wreath of curling smoke ascend from that genteel pipe at the top of the shed. Could it be a chimney, then?

The woman of the lodge, hearing footsteps, came out to her door, already open, hasty words on her tongue.

"Now then! What makes you so late this morning! Didn't I——?" And there she stopped in horror; transfixed; for she had come face to face with the Honourable Mr. Elster.

"Law, sir! *You!* Mercy be good to us!"

He laughed. In her consternation she could only suppose he had dropped from the clouds. A pleasant greeting to her, and then he drew her attention to the appearance that was puzzling him. The woman came out of the door and looked at it.

"*Is* it a chimney, Mrs. Capper?"

"Well yes, sir, it is. Pike have put it in. He come here, nobody knew how or when, and he put hisself into that there old shed, and he have never gone out of it again."

"Who is 'Pike'?" inquired Mr. Elster.

"It's hard to say, sir; a many would give a deal to know. He lay in the shed a bit at first as it were, all open; then he boarded up that there front doorway, and opened a door at the back, and cut out a square hole by it for a winder (you can see 'em both from the rail), and stuck that chimbley in the roof. And there he have lived ever since, and nobody interrupts him. His name's Pike, and that's all that's known. I should think my lord will see to it when he comes."

"Does he work for his living?"

"He never does a stroke o' work for nobody, sir. And how he lives is just one o' them mysteries that can't be dived into. He's a poacher, and a snarer, and a robber of the fish-ponds,—any one of 'em when he gets the chance; leastways it's said he is; and he looks just like a wild man o' the woods, wilder than any Robison Crusoe! And he —— but you might not like me to mention that, sir."

"Mention any thing," replied Mr. Elster. "Go on."

"Well, sir, it's said by some that his was the shot that killed Mr. George," she returned, dropping her voice; and Percival Elster started.

"Who is he?" he exclaimed.

"He is not known to a soul. He came here a stranger."

"But — he was not here when I left home. And I left it, you may remember, but a few days before that night."

"He must have come here at that very time, sir; just as you left."

"But what grounds were there for supposing that he — that he —— I think you must be mistaken, Mrs. Capper. Lord Hartledon, I am sure, knows nothing of this suspicion."

"I never heard nothing about grounds, sir," simply replied the woman. "I suppose folks fastened it on him because he's a loose character: and he have got his face all covered with hair, like a howl."

He nearly laughed again as he turned away, dismissing the suspicion she had hinted at altogether from his mind as unworthy a moment's credit. The broad gravel-walk through this portion of the park was very short, and the large house of gray stone was soon reached. Not to the broad front steps did he bend his course; at that early hour of the morning he might hammer at the door unheard; but turned to a small entrance on the side, and that he found open. Pursuing his way along certain passages, he came to what used to be called the "west kitchen;" and there sat three women at breakfast.

"Well, Mirrable! I thought I should find you up."

The two servants seated opposite to him both stared, with open mouth; neither knew him: the one he had addressed as Mirrable turned short round at the salutation, screamed, and dropped the tea-pot. She was an active thin woman, of forty years, with a bunch of black drooping ringlets hanging between her cap and her thin cheeks, dark eyes, and a ready tongue and pleasant manner. Mirrable had been the upper maid at Hartledon for years and years.

"Mr. Percival! Is it your ghost, sir?"

"I think it's myself, Mirrable."

"My goodness! But, sir, how did you get here?"

"You may well ask. I ought to have been here last night, but got out at some obscure junction to obtain a light for my cigar, and the train went on without me. I sat on a bench for a few hours, and came on by the goods train this morning."

Mirrable awoke from her astonishment to common-sense. She sent the two girls flying, one here, one there, to make rooms ready for Mr. Elster, and busied herself to prepare the best breakfast she could extemporise. Val Elster sat down on a table while he talked to her. In the old days he and his brothers, little fellows, had used to carry their troubles to Mirrable; and he was just as much at home with her now as he would have been with his mother.

"Did Capper see you as you came by, sir? Wouldn't she be struck!"

"Into stone, nearly," he laughed.

Mirrable disappeared for a minute or two, and came back with a silver coffee-pot in her hand. The name of the lodge-keeper had brought to his remembrance the unpleasant hint she mentioned, and he spoke of it on impulse—as he did most things.

"Mirrable, what man is it they call Pike, who has taken possession of that old shed?"

"I'm sure I don't know, sir," answered Mirrable, after a pause, which Mr. Elster thought was involuntary; for she was busy at the moment rubbing the coffee-pot with some wash-leather, her head and face bent over it, as she stood with her back to him before a sort of ironing-board. He stepped off the table, and went up to her.

"I saw smoke arising from the shed, and asked Capper what it meant, and she told me about this Pike. Pike! it's a curious name."

Mirrable rubbed away, never answering.

"Capper said he had been suspected of firing the shot that killed my brother," he continued in a low tone. "Did *you* ever hear of such a hint, Mirrable?"

Mirrable darted off to the fire-place, and began stirring the milk lest it should boil over. But that her face was pretty near buried in the saucepan, Mr. Elster might have seen the sudden change that came over it: the thin cheeks had flushed crimson, and now were deadly white. Lifting the saucepan on the hob to guard against contingencies, she turned round to Mr. Elster.

"Don't you believe any such nonsense, sir," she said; her tone one of strange emphasis. "It was no more Pike than it was me. The man keeps himself to himself, and troubles nobody; and for that very reason idle folks carp at him, like mischief-making idiots as they are!"

"I thought there was nothing in it," remarked Mr. Elster.

"I'm *sure* there isn't," said Mirrable conclusively. "You'd like some broiled ham, sir, wouldn't you?"

"I'd like any thing that's substantial. I'm as hungry as a hunter. But, Mirrable, you don't ask what has brought me here all on a sudden!"

The tone was significant, and Mirrable looked at him. There was a spice of mischief in his laughing blue eyes.

"I come on a mission to you. An avant-courrier from his lordship, to charge you to have things in readiness; for to-morrow you will receive a houseful of company, more than Hartledon will hold."

Mirrable looked aghast. "It is one of your jokes, Mr. Val!"

"Indeed, it is the truth. My brother will be down with a train-full; and he desires that every thing shall be made ready for their reception. It is so, Mirrable."

"My patience!" gasped Mirrable. "And the servants, sir?"

"They will be here to-night, most of them. The Countess Dowager of Kirton is coming as Hartledon's mistress for the time being."

"O," said Mirrable, who had once the honour

of seeing the Countess Dowager of Kirton. And the monosyllable, as applied to that lady, was so significant that Val Elster drew down the corners of his lips.

"I don't like the Countess Dowager, sir," remarked Mirrable in her freedom.

"I can't bear her," said Val Elster.

CHAPTER II.

WILLY GUM.

HAD the Honourable Mr. Elster lingered ever so short a time near the clerk's house that morning, he would have been rewarded by meeting that functionary himself; for in less than a minute after he had passed out of sight, Jabez Gum's door opened, and Jabez Gum glided out of it.

Don't cavil at the word—glided. It is a term that gets applied chiefly to ghosts; and Mr. Gum was a great deal more like a ghost than he was like a man. He was remarkably tall, and remarkably thin; a very shadow, with a thin white shadow of a face, and a nose that was a natural curiosity, and might have made the model of any mask in a carnival of guys. A long thin sharp nose, double the length and only half the thickness of any ordinary nose—a very ferret of a nose; its sharp tip standing straight out into the air. People said, with such a nose Mr. Gum ought to have a great deal of curiosity. And they were right; he *had* a great deal in a quiet way.

A most respectable man was Mr. Gum, and he prided himself upon it. Mr. Gum — called Clerk Gum mostly in the village—had never done a wrong thing in his life, or got into a scrape; he had been altogether a pattern to Calne in general, and to the black sheep of it in particular. Dr. Ashton himself could not have less brought against him than Clerk Gum; and it would just have broken Mr. Gum's heart had his good name been tarnished in ever so slight a degree. Perhaps no man living had been born with a larger share of self-esteem that Jabez Gum. Clerk of the parish longer than Dr. Ashton had been its rector, Jabez Gum had lived at his ease in a pecuniary point of view. It was one of those few parishes (I don't think many of them remain now) where the clerk's emoluments are large. He also held other offices—was an agent for one or two companies, and was looked upon as an exceedingly substantial man for his station in life. Perhaps he was less so than people thought. The old saying is all too true a one—"Nobody knows where the shoe pinches save he who wears it."

Jabez Gum had his thorn, as a great many more of us have ours, if the outside world did but know it. And Jabez, at odd moments, when the thorn pierced him very sharply, had been wont to compare his condition to St. Paul's, and to wonder whether the pricks inflicted on that holy man could have bled as his own did. He meant no irreverence when he thought this; neither do I in writing it. We are generally wounded in the most vulnerable spot about us, and Jabez Gum made no exception; he had been assailed in his cherished respectability, in his self-esteem. Assailed and *scarred*. How broad and deep the scar was, Jabez had never told to the world, which as a rule does not take sympathisingly to such scars, but shakes them off in its cruel indifference. The world had nearly for-

gotten the scar now, and supposed Clerk Gum
had done the same; it was all over and done
with years ago.

Jabez Gum's wife—to whom you will have
the honour of an introduction shortly, but she's in
her bed-room just now—had borne him one child,
and only one. How this boy was loved, how
tenderly he was brought up, let Calne tell you.
Mrs. Gum had to endure no inconsiderable amount
of ridicule at the time from her gossiping friends,
who gave Willy sundry names—the swan, the
lambkin, the love, all applied in derision. Certainly if any mother ever was bound up in a
child, Mrs. Gum was in hers. The boy was
brought up well: a good education was given to
him; and at the age of sixteen he went to London and to fortune: the one was looked upon as
a natural sequence of the other. Some friend of
Jabez Gum's had interested himself to procure
the lad admission into one of the great banks
there as junior clerk; he might rise in time to be
its cashier, its manager, even its partner, who
knew? Who knew indeed? and Clerk Gum

congratulated himself, and was more respectable than ever.

Better that Willy Gum had remained at Calne! And yet, and again—who knew? Where the propensity to ill-doing exists, it is sure to come out, no matter where. There were some people in Calne who could have told Clerk Gum, even then, that Willy, for his age, was tolerably fast and forward. Mrs. Gum had heard of one or two things that had caused her hair to rise on end with horror; ay, and with apprehension; but, foolish mother that she was, not a syllable did she breathe to the clerk, and nobody else ventured to tell him. She talked to Willy imploringly, with many sobs and tears — that he would be a good boy and enter on good courses, not on bad ones, and not break her heart. Willy, the little scapegoat, was willing to promise anything; he laughed and made light of it; it wasn't his fault if folks told stories of him; she shouldn't be so foolish as to give ear to them. London? O, he should be all right in London! One or two fellows here were rather fast, there was no denying it; and they drew him with them; they were older than himself, and ought to have known better. Once away from Calne, they could have no more influence over him, and he should be all right. She believed him; she put faith in the plausible words. O, what trust can be so pure, and at the same time so foolish, as that placed by a mother in a beloved son! Mrs. Gum had never known but one idol on earth,—he who now stood before her, lightly laughing at her fears, and making his own tale good. She leaned forward and laid her hands upon his shoulders and kissed him with that impassioned fervour that some mothers could tell of, and whispered that she would trust him wholly. Mr. Willy extricated himself with as little impatience as he could help: these embraces were not to his taste. And yet the boy did love his mother: she was not at all a wise woman, or a clever one; rather silly indeed in many things; but she was fond of him. At this period he was young-looking for his age, slight, and rather undersized, with an exceedingly light complexion, a wishy-washy sort of face with no colour in it, unmeaning light eyes, white eyebrows, and ragged-looking light hair with a tawny shade over it.

Willy Gum departed for London, and entered on his engagement in the great banking-house of Goldsworthy and Co. How he went on in it, Calne could not get to know, though it was moderately inquisitive upon the point. His father and mother heard from him occasionally, and once the clerk took a sudden and rather mysterious journey to London, where he stayed for a whole week. Rumour said—I wonder where such rumours first get their rise—that Willy Gum had got into some trouble, and the clerk had had to buy him out of it at the cost of a mint of money. The clerk, however, gave no confirmation of this; and one thing was indisputable: Willy retained his place in the banking-house. Some people looked on this fact as a complete refutation of the rumour.

Then came a lull. Nothing was heard of Willy; that is, nothing beyond the reports of Mrs. Gum to her gossips, when letters arrived—that he was well, and getting on well. It was only the lull that precedes a storm; and a storm indeed burst on quiet Calne. Willy Gum had robbed the bank and disappeared.

In the first dreadful moment, perhaps, the only one who did *not* disbelieve it was Clerk Gum. Other people said there must be some mistake—that it could not be. Kind old Lord Hartledon came down in his carriage to the clerk's house—he was ailing; too ill to walk—and sat with the clerk and the weeping mother, and said he was sure it could not be so bad as was reported. The next morning saw handbills—great, staring, large-typed handbills—offering a reward for the discovery of the thief, William Gum, stuck up all over Calne.

Once more Clerk Gum went to London. What he did there, nobody knew; one only thing was certain—he did not find Willy or any trace of him. The defalcation was very nearly eight hundred pounds; and even if Mr. Gum could have refunded that large sum, he might not, said Calne, for of course the bank would not compound a felony. He came back looking ten years older;

his tall thin form was more shadowy, his nose was longer and sharper. Not a soul ventured to say a syllable to him, even of condolence. He told Lord Hartledon and his rector that no tidings whatever could be gleaned of his unhappy son; the boy had disappeared, and might be dead, for all they knew to the contrary.

So the handbills wore themselves out on the walls, serving no purpose, until Lord Hartledon ordered them to be torn down; and Mrs. Gum lived in tears, and audibly wished she was dead. She had not seen her boy since he quitted Calne, considerably more than two years before, and he was now nearly nineteen. A few days' holiday had been accorded him by the banking-house each Christmas; but the first Christmas Willy wrote word that he had accepted an invitation to go home with a brother-clerk; the second Christmas he said he could not get leave of absence— which Mrs. Gum afterwards found was untrue; so that Willy Gum had not been at Calne since he quitted it. And whenever his mother thought of him—and that was every hour of the day and night—it was always as the fair, young, light-haired boy, who seemed to her little more than a child.

A year or so of uncertainty, of suspense, of wailing, and then came a letter from Willy, sent cautiously. It was not addressed direct to Mrs. Gum, to whom it was written, but to some one of Willy's acquaintances in London, who enclosed it in an envelope and forwarded it on. Such a letter! To read it, one might have thought Mr. William Gum had gone out under the most fashionable auspices. He was in Australia; had gone up to try his fortune at the gold diggings, and was making money rapidly. In a short while he should refund with interest the little sum he had borrowed from Goldsworthy and Co., and which was really not taken with any ill intention, but was more of an accident than otherwise. After that, he should accumulate money on his own score, and—all things being made straight at home—come back and settle down, a rich man for life. And she—his mother—might *rely* on his keeping his word. At present he was at Melbourne; to which place he and his mates had come to bring their acquired gold, and to take a bit of a spree for their recent hard labour. He was very jolly; and after a week's holiday they should go back again. And he hoped his father had overlooked the past; and he remained ever her affectionate son, William Gum.

The effect of this letter upon Mrs. Gum was as if a dark pall had suddenly been lifted from the world, to give place to a flood of golden sunshine. We estimate things by comparison. Mrs. Gum was by nature disposed to look on the dark side of objects, and she had for the whole past year been indulging the most dread pictures of Willy and his fate that any woman's mind ever conceived. To hear that he was in life, and well, and making money rapidly, and withal "jolly," was the sweetest news she had ever tasted, the greatest relief she could experience in this world. Clerk Gum—relieved also no doubt—received the tidings in a more sober spirit, almost as if he did not dare to believe in them: the man's heart had been well-nigh broken with the blow that fell upon him, and nothing could ever heal it thoroughly again. He read the letter in silence; read it twice over; and when his wife broke out in a series of rapt congratulations, and reproached him mildly for not appearing to think it true, he rather cynically inquired what then, if true, became of her dreams.

For Mrs. Gum was a dreamer. She was one of those who are now and again visited by strange dreams, significant of the future; not often it may be, once or twice in their lifetime. Poor Mrs. Gum carried these dreams to an excess; that is, she was always having them and always talking of them. It had been no wonder, with her mind in the miserable state it was, in regard to her son, that her dreams in that first twelvemonth had mostly been of him and mostly bad. The above question, put by her husband, somewhat puzzled her; her dreams *had* foreshadowed great ill still to Willy; and her dreams had never been wrong yet.

But, in the enjoyment of actual good, who thinks of dreams? Nobody. And Mrs. Gum's grew a shade brighter, and hope again took possession of her heart. Two years rolled on, during which they heard twice from Willy; satisfactory letters still, in a way. Both testified to his "jolly" state: he was getting rich, though not quite so rapidly as he had anticipated; a fellow had to spend so much! Every day he expected to pick up a thumping big nugget, which would crown his fortune. He complained in these letters that he did not hear from home; not once had news reached him; had his father and mother abandoned him? The question brought forth a gush of tears from Mrs. Gum, and a sharp abuse of the post-office. The clerk took the news philosophically, remarking that the wonder would have been had Willy got the letters, seeing that he seemed to move about incessantly from place to place. Close upon this came another letter from him, written apparently in haste. Willy's "fortune" had turned into reality at last; he was coming home with more gold than he could count; had taken his berth in the good ship Morning Star, and should come off at once to Calne, when the ship reached Liverpool. There was a line written inside the envelope, as if he had forgotten to put it in the letter: "I have had one from you at last; the first you wrote, it seems. Thank old dad for what he has done for me; I'll make it all square with him when I get home."

This had reference to a fact which Calne did not know. In that unhappy second visit of Clerk Gum's to London, he *did* succeed in appeasing the wrath of Goldsworthy and Co., and paid in every farthing of the money. How far he might have accomplished this, but for being backed by the urgent influence of old Lord Hartledon, was a question. One thing was in his favour,—the firm had not taken any public steps whatever in the matter, and those handbills circulated at Calne were the result of a misapprehension on the part of an officious local police-officer. Things had not gone too far for Goldsworthys graciously to condone the offence—and Clerk Gum paid in his savings of years. This was the fact written by Mrs. Gum to her son, which had called forth the few words of the envelope.

Alas! those were the last tidings ever received from Willy Gum. While Mrs. Gum lived in a state of ecstasy, showing the letter of good news incessantly to her neighbours, and making loving preparation for his reception, the time for the arrival of the Morning Star at Liverpool drew on, and passed, and the ship did not come. A space of anxious suspense, of mourning for her by all who had relations on board—for it was supposed she had foundered at sea—and tidings arrived. An awful tale—a tale of mutiny and wrong and bloodshed. Some of the loose characters on board the ship—and she was bringing home such—had risen in disorder within a month of their sailing from Melbourne; had killed the captain, the chief officer, and some of the crew and passengers. The ringleader was a man of the name of Gordon; he it was who had incited the rest to the crime, and he had killed the captain with his own hand. Obtaining command of the ship, they put her about, and commenced a raid of piracy. One vessel they succeeded in disarming, in despoiling, and then in leaving her to her fate; but the next vessel they attacked proved a formidable enemy, and there was a hand-to-hand struggle for the mastery, and for life or death. The Morning Star was sunk, with the greater portion of her live freight; a few, only some four or five, were saved by the other ship, and conveyed home to England. It was by them the dark tale was brought. The second officer of the Morning Star was one; he had been compelled to dissemble and to appear to serve the mutinous band; the others were innocent passengers, whose lives had not been taken. All these agreed in one thing: that Gordon, the ringleader, had in all probability escaped. He had been seen to put off from the Morning Star, when she was sinking, in one of her best boats; he and some of his lawless helpmates, with a bag of biscuit, a cask of water, and a few bottles that probably contained rum. Whether they would succeed in reaching a port, or in getting picked up, was a question; but it was assumed they would. The owners of the Morning Star, half paralysed at the news of so daring and unusual an outrage, offered the large reward of five hundred pounds for the capture of George Gordon; and government increased the offer by two hundred, making it seven.

Overwhelming tidings for Clerk Gum and his wife! There ensued a brief season of agonised suspense for the poor mother; of hopes and fears as to whether Willy was among the poor remnant saved; and then hope died away, for he did not come. Once more, for the last time, Clerk Gum took a journey, not to London, but to Liverpool. He succeeded in seeing the officer who had been saved; but that gentleman could give him no information. He knew the names of the first-class passengers, but only a few of the second-class; and in that class Willy had most likely sailed. The clerk described his son; and the officer thought he remembered him: he had a good deal of gold on board, he said. One of the passengers spoke more positively. Yes, by Clerk Gum's description, he was sure Willy Gum had been his fellow-passenger in the second cabin, though he did not recollect whether he had heard his name — it seemed, looking back, that the passengers had hardly had time to get acquainted with each other's names, he said. He was sure it was the young man; very light in complexion, ready and rather loose (if Mr. Gum would excuse his saying so) in speech. He had made thorough good hauls of gold at the last, and was going home to spend it. He was the second killed, poor fellow; he had risen up with a volley of oaths (excuses begged again) to defend the captain, and was struck down and killed. Poor Jabez Gum gasped. *Killed?* was the gentleman *sure?* Quite sure; and, moreover, he saw his body thrown overboard with the rest of the dead. And the money—the gold? Jabez asked, when he had somewhat recovered himself. The passenger laughed—not at the poor father, but at the worse than useless question: gold and every thing else that had been aboard the Morning Star went down with her to the bottom of the sea. A sort of savage impulse rose in the clerk's mind, replacing his first shock of grief; an impulse that might almost have led him to murder the villain Gordon, could he have come across him. Was there a chance that he'd be taken, that man? he asked. Every chance, if he dared show his face in England, the passenger answered: a reward of seven hundred pounds was an inducement to the survivors to keep their eyes open; and they'd do it, besides, without any reward. Moreover—if Gordon had escaped, his comrades in the boat had escaped with him; they were lawless men like himself, every one of them, and they would be sure to betray him when they found what a price was set upon his capture.

Clerk Gum returned home, bearing to his wife and to Calne the final tidings which crushed out all hope. Mrs. Gum sank into a state of wild despair; at first it almost seemed to threaten loss of reason: her son had been her sole idol, and the idol was shattered. But to witness unreasonably violent grief in others always has a counteracting effect on our own, and Mr. Gum soothed his sorrow and brought philosophy to his aid.

"Look you," said he, one day, sharply to his wife, when she was crying and moaning, "there's two sides to every calamity,—a bright un and a dark un;" for Mr. Gum was not in the habit of treating his wife, in the privacy of their domestic circle, to the quality-speech kept for the world. "He is gone, and we can't help it; we'd have welcomed him home if we could, and killed the fatted calf, but it was God's will that it shouldn't be. There may be a blessing in it, after all: who knows but he might have broke out again, and brought upon us what he did afore, or worse? For my part, I should never have been without the fear; night and morning it would always have stood before me prominent; not to be drove away. As it is, I be at rest."

She—the wife—took her apron from her eyes and looked at him; looked at him in a sort of amazed anger.

"Gum! do you forget that he had left off his ills, and was coming home to comfort us?"

"No, I don't forget it," returned Mr. Gum.

"But who was to answer for it that the mood would last? He might have got through his gold, however much it was, and then —— As it is, Nance Gum, we can sleep quiet in our beds, free from *that* fear."

Clerk Gum was not, on the whole, a model of suavity in the domestic fold: the first blow which had fallen upon him seemed to have touched his temper; and his helpmate knew from experience that whenever he called her "Nance" his mood was at its worst.

Swallowing down a heavy sob, she spoke reproachfully:

"It's my firm belief, Gum, and has been all along, that you cared more for your good name among men than you did for the boy."

"Perhaps I did," he answered, by way of retort. "At any rate, it might have been better for him in the long-run if we — both you and me — hadn't cared for him quite so foolishly in his childhood; we spared the rod, and we spoiled the child. That's over, and—"

"It's *all* over," interrupted Mrs. Gum with

a sob; "over for ever in this world. Gum, you be very hard-hearted."

"And," he continued, with a composure as if there had been no interruption, "we may hope now to live it down in time, that blow he brought upon us, and hold up our heads again in the face of Calne. We couldn't have done that while he lived."

"We couldn't?"

"No. Just dry up your useless tears, Nancy; and get to think that all's for the best."

But, metaphorically speaking, Mrs. Nancy Gum could not dry her tears. Nearly two years had elapsed since the fatal event; and though she no longer lamented openly, filling Calne with her cries and her faint but heart-felt prayers for vengeance on the head of the cruel monster, George Gordon, as she used to do at first, she had sunk into a despairing state of mind by no means desirable: a startled, timid, superstitious woman she was now, frightened at every shadow.

CHAPTER III.

ANNE ASHTON.

JABEZ GUM, tall and thin and shadowy, came out of his house in the brightness of the summer morning, missing by one minute only the Honourable Mr. Elster. He went round to a small shed at the back of the house and brought forth sundry garden-tools. The whole of the garden was kept in order by himself, and nobody had finer fruit and vegetables than Clerk Gum. Hartledon might be proud of them, and Dr. Ashton sometimes accepted a dish with pleasure.

In his present attire,—dark trousers, and a short close dark jacket, like a schoolboy's, which he buttoned up round him, and generally wore in gardening,—the worthy man might decidedly have been taken for a galvanised lamppost, by any stranger who should happen to come by. He was applying himself this morning, first to the nailing-up of sundry choice fruit-trees against the wall that ran along one side of his garden — a wall that had been erected by the clerk himself in happier days—and next, to the plucking of some green walnuts for his wife to pickle. As he stood on tiptoe, his long thin body and his long thin arms stretched up to the walnut-tree, he might have made the fortune of any travelling caravan that could have hired him. The very few people who passed called out to him the good-morrow, but he rarely turned his head in answering them. Clerk Gum had grown somewhat taciturn to the world of late years.

The time went on. The clock struck a quarter-past seven, and Jabez Gum, as he heard it, quitted the walnut-tree, walked to the gate, and leaned over it; his face turned in the direction of the village. It was not a common wooden gate, as is generally seen to smaller houses in rustic localities, but a very pretty iron one; every thing about the clerk's house was superior. Apparently, he was looking out for some one in displeasure; and, indeed, he had not stood there a minute, when a girl came flying along the road, and pushed the gate and the clerk back together. She was habited in a blue-cotton gown, an old rag of a shawl, and a broken straw bonnet; a wild-looking, saucy gipsy of a girl, whose black hair had come down her back on the road.

Mr. Gum twisted her round by the shoulders, and directed her attention to the church clock. "Do you see the time, Becca Jones?"

Had the pages of the church-register been visible as well as the clock, Miss Rebecca Jones's age might have been seen to be fifteen; but, in knowledge of the world and impudence, or, as the village was in the habit of putting it, "brass," she was considerably older.

"Just gone seven and a quarter," answered she, making a feint of shading her eyes with her two hands, though the sun was behind her.

"And what business have you to come at seven and a quarter? Half-past six is your time; and if you can't keep to it, your missis will get those that can?"

"Why can't my missis let me stop at night and clear up the work?" returned the girl. "She sends me away at six o'clock, as soon as I've washed the tea-things, and oftentimes earlier than that, afore tea's been had at all. It stands to reason I can't get through the work of a morning."

"You could get through it quite well if you came to time," said the clerk, turning away to his walnut-tree. "Why don't you?"

"I overslep' myself this morning. Father never called me afore he went out. He got a drop last night, I expect; I heard mother a-screeching at him."

She went flying up the gravel-path as she spoke, dashing her cotton gown on the flowers on either side it. Her father was the Mr. Jones whom you saw at the railway-station; her stepmother (for her own mother was dead) was Mrs. Gum's cousin. She was a sort of stray sheep, this girl, in the eyes of Calne, not belonging very much to any body; her father habitually neglected her, her step-mother had twice turned her out of doors. Some three or four months back, when Mrs. Gum was changing her servant, she had consented to try this girl as one. Jabez Gum knew nothing of the arrangement until it was concluded, and he disapproved of it. Altogether, it did not work satisfactorily: Miss Jones was careless, idle, very free in speech; her step-mother was dissatisfied because she was not taken into the house; and Clerk Gum threatened every day, and his wife sometimes, to turn the girl off. It was only within a year or two that they had not kept a regular indoor servant; and the fact of their not doing so puzzled the gossips of Calne: the clerk's emoluments were the same as ever; there was no Willy to encroach on them now; and the work of the house required a good servant. However, it pleased Mrs. Gum to have one in only by day; and who was to interfere, if the clerk did not?

Jabez Gum worked on, worked on for some little time after eight o'clock, the breakfast-hour; he rather wondered he was not called to it, and made a mental vow to discharge Miss Becca. Presently he went indoors, put his head into a small sitting-room on the left, and found the room empty, but the breakfast laid. The kitchen was behind it, and Jabez Gum stalked on down the passage, which ran right through the house to the back-door, and went into the kitchen. On the other side the passage was the best sitting-room, looking front, and a very small room at the back of it, which Jabez used as an office, and kept sundry account-books in.

"Where's your missis?" asked he of the maid, who was on her knees toasting a piece of bread.

"Ain't down yet," was the short response.

"Not down yet!" repeated Jabez in surprise, for Mrs. Gum was generally down by seven. "You've got that door open again, Becca! How many more times am I to tell you I won't have it?"

"It's the smoke," said Becca; "this chimbley's always a-smoking when it's first lighted."

"The chimbley's not, and you know that you are telling a falsehood. What do you want with it open? You'll have that wild man dart in upon you some morning. How'll you like that?"

"I ain't afeard of him," was the answer, as

Becca got up from her knees, and proceeded to scratch at the toast with a knife, for she had burnt it. "He couldn't eat me."

"But you know how timid your mistress is of him," returned the clerk in a voice of exceeding anger. "How dare you, girl, be insolent?"

He shut the door as he spoke—one that opened from the kitchen to the garden at the back—and bolted it. Washing his hands at the sink, and drying them with the round towel hanging at the scullery door, he went upstairs, and found Mrs. Gum—as he did now and then find her of late—in a sort of prostration. She was a little woman, with a light complexion, insipid unmeaning face—some such a face as Willy's had been—and her hair, worn in neat bands under her cap, was the colour of light rope.

"I couldn't help it, Gum," she began, as she stood before the glass, her trembling fingers trying to fasten her black alpacca gown,—for she had never put off the mourning for their son. "It's past eight, I know; but I've had such a upset this morning that never was, and I *couldn't* dress myself. I had a shocking dream."

"Drat your dreams!" irascibly cried Mr. Gum, very much wanting his breakfast.

"Ah, Gum, don't! Them morning dreams, when they be vivid as this was, are not sent for ridicule. Pike was in it; and you know I *can't bear* him to be in my dreams. They are bad always when he is in them."

"If you wanted your breakfast as bad as I want it, you'd let Pike alone," retorted the clerk.

"I thought he was mixed up in some business with Lord Hartledon. I don't know what it was, but the dream was full of horror. It seemed that Lord Hartledon was dead or dying; whether he'd been killed or not, I can't say; but an awful dread was upon me of seeing him, and seeing him dead. A voice called out, 'Don't let him come to Calne!' and in the fright I awoke. I can't remember what part Pike had in the dream," she continued in self-soliloquy; "the impression remained that he was in it."

"Perhaps he killed Lord Hartledon?" interrupted Gum, in mocking retort.

"No; that I am certain he did not; not in the

dream, you understand. Pike did not seem to be mixed in it for ill. The ill was all on Lord Hartledon; but it was not Pike brought it to him. Who it was did it, I couldn't see; but it was not Pike."

Clerk Gum looked down at his wife; amazement, blended with a sort of scornful pity, in his face. He wondered sometimes, in his phlegmatic reason, why women were created such fools.

"Look you here, Mrs. G. I thought them dreams of yours were pretty nigh dreamt out—there have been enough of 'em. How any woman, short of a born idiot, can stand there and confess herself frighted by a dream such as that, so as to be unable to get up and go about her duties, is beyond me. I'd steady my hands and legs with weights, afore they should tremble as yours be trembling."

"But, Gum, you don't let me finish. I woke up with the horror, I tell you—"

"What horror?" spoke the clerk again, too angry to let her go on without contradiction. "Where was the horror? What did it consist of? I can't see it."

"No more can I, very clear," acknowledged Mrs. Gum; "but I know it was there. I woke up, Gum, with the very words in my ears, 'Don't let him come to Calne!' and I started out of bed in terror for Lord Hartledon, lest he should come. We are only half awake, you know, at them moments. I pulled aside the dimity curtain and looked out; any thing for company. Gum, if ever I thought to drop in all my life, I thought it then. There was but one person to be seen at all in the road—a gentleman; and it was Lord Hartledon."

"O!" said Mr. Gum cynically, after a moment's pause of natural surprise. "Come out of his vault in the church, close by, to take a morning walk past your window, Mrs. G.!"

"Church vault! I mean the young Lord Hartledon, Gum."

Mr. Gum was a little taken aback. They had been so much in the habit of calling the present Earl, Lord Elster, and who had not lived at Calne since he came into the title, that he had thought of the old lord all the time his wife was speaking.

"He was up there, just by the turning of the

road, going on seemingly to Hartledon. Gum, I nearly dropped, I say. The next minute he was out of sight; then I rubbed my eyes and pinched my arms to make sure whether I was awake."

"And whether you saw a ghost, or whether you didn't," came the mocking comment.

"It was not a ghost, Gum; it was Lord Hartledon himself."

"Nonsense! It was just as much one as it was the t'other. The fact is, you haven't quite woke up out of that fine dream of yours, Mrs. G., and you saw double. It was just as much young Hartledon as it was me."

"I never see a ghost yet, and I don't fear I ever shall, Gum. I tell you it was Lord Hartledon. And if some harm doesn't befal him at Calne, as was shadowed forth in my dream, never you believe me again."

"There, that's enough," peremptorily cried the clerk; knowing, if once Mrs. Gum took up any notion that had a dream for its basis, how impossible it was to turn her. "Is the key of that kitchen back-door found yet?"

"No: it never will be, Gum. I've told you so afore. My belief is, and always have been, that Becca let it drop by accident into the swilltub."

"*My* belief is, that Becca made away with it for her own purposes," said the clerk with a significant sniff. "I caught her now with the door stark-staring open. She's trying to make acquaintance with that Pike; that's what she's at."

"O, Gum!"

"Yes; it's all very well to say 'O, Gum;' but if you were below-stairs looking after her, instead of dreaming above 'em, it might be better. Let me once get at a certainty about it, and she goes off the next hour. A fine thing it 'll be some day for us to find her head down'ards, smothered in the kitchen purgatory, and the silver spoons gone; as 'll be the case if any loose characters get in."

He was descending the stairs as he spoke the last sentence, which was delivered in a loud tone, probably for the benefit of Miss Becca Jones. And lest the intelligent Protestant reader should fear he is being introduced to unorthodox regions, it may be as well to mention that the " purgatory" in Mr. Jabez Gum's kitchen consisted of a hole, two feet square, under the hearth, covered with a grating, through which the ashes and the small cinders fell; thereby enabling the economical housewife to throw the larger ones on the fire again: such holes being common enough in the old-fashioned kitchens of some English districts, as is their appellation, the " purgatory."

Mrs. Gum, ready now, had been about to follow her husband; but his suggestion—that the girl was watching an opportunity to make acquaintance with their undescribable neighbour, Pike—struck her motionless. It seemed that she could never see this man without a twitter; could not overcome the fright experienced when she first met him. It was on a dark autumn night. She was coming through the garden when she discerned, or thought she discerned, a light in the unused shed. Thinking of fire, she hastily crossed the stile that divided their garden from the bit of waste land, and ran to it. There she was confronted by what she took to be a bear—but a bear that could talk; for he gruffly asked her who she was and what she wanted. A black-haired, black-browed man, with a pipe between his teeth, and one sinewy arm bared to the elbow. How Mrs. Gum tore away and tumbled over the stile again in her terror, and got home, she never knew. She supposed it was a tramp, who had but taken shelter there for the night; but she found to her dismay that the tramp stayed on, and she had never overcome her fright from that hour to this. Neither did her husband like the proximity of such a gentleman: they caused securer bolts to be put on their doors—for fastenings in small country places are not much cared for, people around being proverbially honest. They also had their shutters altered. The shutters to the windows, back and front, previously had holes in them in the form of a heart, such as you may have sometimes noticed: before the wild-looking man—whose name came to be known as Pike—had been in possession of the shed a fortnight, Jabez Gum had the holes in his shutters filled-in and painted over. An additional security, said the neighbours: but poor timid Mrs. Gum could not overcome that first fright, and the very mention of the man sent her into a tremble.

Nothing more was said of the dream or the apparition, real or fancied, of the Earl of Hartledon: Clerk Gum did not encourage the familiar mention of topics so unsubstantial in everyday life. He took his breakfast, devoted an hour to his own business in the little office, and then put on his coat to go out. It was Friday morning. On that day and on Wednesdays the church was open for baptisms, and it was the clerk's custom to go over at ten o'clock and apprise the rector of any notices he might have had.

Passing in at the iron gates, the beautiful white house rose before him, across the extensive green-velvet lawn. It had been built by Dr. Ashton at his own cost: the old rectory was a tumble-down, inconvenient place, always in dilapidation, for as soon as one part of it was repaired, another fell through; and the rector opened his heart and his purse, both large and generous, and built a new one. Mr. Gum was making his way, unannounced, to the rector's study, as was his custom, when a door at the opposite side of the hall opened, and Dr. Ashton looked out. He was a pleasant-looking man, with dark hair and eyes, his countenance one of keen intellect; and though only of middle height, there was something stately, grand, imposing in his whole appearance.

"Is that you, Jabez?"

Connected with each other so many years— connection which had begun when both were young—the rector and Mrs. Ashton had never called him any thing but Jabez. With other people he was Gum, or Mr. Gum, or Clerk Gum: Jabez with them. He, Jabez, was the older man of the two by six or seven years, for the rector was not more than forty-five. The clerk crossed the hall, its tessellated flags gleaming under the colours thrown in by the bright painted windows, and entered the drawing-room; a noble apartment looking on to the lawn in front. Mrs. Ashton, a tall delicate-looking woman, with a gentle face, was standing before a painting just come home and hung up; to look at which had taken the rector and his wife into the room.

It was a portrait. A sweet-looking girl with a smiling countenance, a sunny face. The features were of the delicate contour of Mrs. Ashton's; the rich brown hair, the soft brown eyes, and the sensible and intellectual expression of face resembled the doctor's. Altogether, the face and the portrait were positively charming; one of the faces you must love at first sight, without thinking to question whether or not they are beautiful.

"Is it like, Jabez?" asked the rector, while Mrs. Ashton made room for him with a smile of greeting.

"As like as two peas, sir," responded Jabez, when he had taken a moment's look. "What a face it is! Oftentimes it comes across my mind when I am not thinking of any thing but business; and I'm always the better for it."

"Why, Jabez, this is the first time you have seen it."

"Ah, ma'am, you know I mean the original. There's two baptisms to-day, sir," he added, turning away; "two, and one churching,—Mrs. Luttrell and her child, and the poor little baby whose mother died."

"Mrs. Luttrell!" repeated the rector. "It's very early for her, is it not?"

"They want to go away to the sea-side," replied the clerk. "What about that notice, sir?"

"I'll see about it before Sunday, Jabez. Any news?"

"No, sir; not that I've heard of. My wife wanted to persuade me that she saw—"

At this moment a white-haired old serving-man entered the room with a note, calling off the rector's attention. "The man's to take back the answer, sir, if you please."

"Wait then, Simon."

Old Simon stood aside, his waiter in his hand, and the clerk resumed to Mrs. Ashton the sentence he had broken off to the rector.

"She wanted to persuade me she saw young Lord Hartledon pass at six o'clock, or so, this morning. A very likely tale that, ma'am."

"Perhaps she dreamt it, Jabez," said Mrs. Ashton quietly.

Jabez chuckled; but what he would have answered was interrupted by the old man.

"It's Mr. Elster that's come; not Lord Hartledon."

"Mr. Elster come! How do you know it, Simon?" quickly asked Mrs. Ashton.

"The gardener mentioned it, ma'am, when he brought in the garden-stuff just now," was the servant's reply. "He said he saw Mr. Elster walk by this morning, as if he had just come by the luggage-train. I'm not sure but he spoke to him."

"Simon, the answer is 'No,'" interposed the rector, in allusion to the letter he had been reading. "But you can send word that I'll call in some time to-day."

"Charles, did you hear what Simon said—that Mr. Elster has come?" asked Mrs. Ashton.

"Yes, I heard it," replied the doctor; and there was a hard dry tone in his voice, as if the news were not altogether palatable to him. "It must have been Percival Elster your wife saw, then, Jabez; not Lord Hartledon."

Jabez had just been sensibly arriving at the same conclusion. "They used to be much alike in height and figure," he observed; "it was easy to mistake the one for the other. Then that's all this morning, sir?"

"There's nothing more, Jabez."

In a room whose large French window opened to some flower-beds on the side of the house, bending over a table on which sundry maps were spread, her face very close to them, sat at this moment a young lady. It was the same sweet face you have just seen in the portrait—that of Dr. and Mrs. Ashton's only daughter. The wondrously sunny expression of countenance, blended with strange sweetness, was even more conspicuous than in the portrait; but what perhaps struck a beholder most, when looking on Miss Ashton for the first time, was a nameless grace and refinement that pervaded her whole appearance. She was of middle height, not more; slender; her head well set upon her shoulders. This was her own room; the school-room of her girlhood, the sitting-room that she had been allowed to call her own since. Books, and work, and music, and a drawing-easel, and various other items, presenting a rather untidy whole, met the eye. This morning it was particularly untidy: the charts covered the table; one of them lay on the carpet; and a little pot of mignonette had been overturned inside the open window. She was very busy: the open sleeves of her lilac-muslin dress were thrown back, and her delicate hands were putting the finishing touches in pencil to a plan she had been drawing, or rather copying from one of the maps. A few minutes more, and the pencil was thrown down in glee.

"I won't begin to colour it this morning; an hour and a half, I'm sure, I have been at it already; but the worst is done, and that's worth a jubilee." In the relief from work, in the innocent gaiety of her heart, she burst forth into a song, and began waltzing round the room to its tune. Barely had she passed the open window, and had her back turned to it, when a gentleman came up, looked in, stepped softly over the threshold, together with the fallen flower-pot, and imprisoned her by the waist.

"Be quiet, Arthur. Pick up that mignonette-pot you threw down, sir. I won't."

"My darling!" came the low, heartfelt, answering whisper. And Miss Ashton, with a faint cry, turned to see her engaged lover, Val Elster. She stood before him, literally unable to speak in her great astonishment, the red rose going and coming in her delicate cheeks, the rich brown eyes, that might have been too brilliant but for their exceeding sweetness, raised, questioning, to his. Mr. Elster folded her in his arms as if he would never release her again, and kissed repeatedly the shrinking face.

"O Percival, Percival! Don't! Let me go."

He let her go at last, and held her before him, her eyelids drooping now, to gaze at the face he loved so well—yes, loved fervently and well, in spite of his follies and his sins. Her heart was beating wildly with its own rapture: for her the world had suddenly become brighter.

"But when did you come?" she whispered, scarcely knowing how to speak the words, in her excess of happiness.

He took her upon his arm and began to pace the room with her while he explained. There was an attempt at excuse for his prolonged absence—for Val Elster had returned from his duties at Vienna in May, and now it was August, and he had lingered the intervening time in London, enjoying himself—but that was soon glossed over; and he told her how his brother was coming down on the morrow with a large number of guests, and he, Val, had offered to precede them and give the necessary instructions at Hartledon. He did not say *why* he had offered; that his debts had become so pressing he was afraid to show himself longer in London: such facts were not for the ear of that fair girl, who trusted him as the truest man she knew under heaven.

"What have you been doing, Anne?"

He was pointing to the table and the maps. Miss Ashton laughed. "Mrs. Graves was here yesterday: she is very clever, you know; and when something was being said about the course of ships out of England, I made some dreadful mistakes; she took me up sharply, and papa looked at me sharply—and the result *is*, I have to do a heap of maps. Please tell me if it's right, Percival?"

She held up to him her pencilled work of the morning. He was laughing.

"What mistakes did you make, Anne?"

"I am not sure; but I said something about an Indiaman, leaving the London Docks, having to pass Scarborough," she said demurely. "It was quite as bad."

"Do you remember, Anne, being punished for persisting, in spite of the big slate on the wall and your nursery governess, that the Mediterranean sea lay between Scotland and Ireland? Miss Jevons wanted to give you bread-and-water for a week. How's that prig Graves?" he added rather abruptly.

Anne Ashton laughed, blushing slightly. "He is just as you left him; very painstaking and efficient in the parish, and all that, but O so stupid in some things! Is the map right?"

"Yes, it's right. I'll help you with the rest. If Dr. Ashton—"

"Why, Val! Is it you? Well, I heard Lord Hartledon had come down."

Percival Elster turned. A lad of seventeen

had come bounding in at the window. It was Dr. Ashton's eldest living son, Arthur. Anne was twenty-one. A son, who would have been nineteen now, had died; and there was another, John, two years younger than Arthur.

"How are you, Arthur boy?" cried Val. "Edward's not come. Who told you he was?"

"Mother Gum. I have just met her."

"She told you wrong. He will be down to-morrow. There's Dr. Ashton!"

Attracted perhaps by the voices, Dr. and Mrs. Ashton, who were then out on the lawn, came round to the window. Percival Elster grasped a hand of each, and after a minute or two's studied coldness, the doctor thawed. It was next to impossible to resist the genial manner, the winning attractions of the young man to his face; but Dr. Ashton could not approve of his line of conduct; and he had sore doubts whether he had done right in allowing him to become the betrothed of his dearly-loved daughter.

CHAPTER IV.

THE COUNTESS DOWAGER.

THE guests had come. The crowd which the young Lord Hartledon had sent his brother, as avant-courrier, to give notice of, had arrived, and Hartledon was alive with bustle and with lights. The first link in the chain, whose fetters were to bind more than one victim, had been forged, and was already linking itself with the next. Link upon link, link upon link; an awful, heavy, despairing weight of burden, which no hand could lift, and which would have to be borne for the most part in dread secrecy and silence.

Mirrable had exerted herself to a purpose, and Mirrable was capable of it when occasion needed. Help had been procured at once from Calne, and on the Friday evening several of the Hartledon servants arrived from the town-house.

"None but a young man would have put us to such a rout," quoth Mirrable in her freedom; "my lord and my lady would have sent a week's notice at least." But when the young man, Lord Hartledon, arrived on the Saturday evening with his guests, Mirrable was ready for them.

She stood at the entrance to receive them, in her rustling black-silk gown, in her plain, good cap of real lace, its broad white-satin strings hanging on either side the bunch of black ringlets that shaded her thin face. Who, to look at her quick sharp countenance, with its good practical sense, her active frame, her ready speech, her capability altogether, would believe that she was sister to that silly, dreaming Mrs. Gum? But it was so. Lord Hartledon, kind, affable, unaffected as ever was his brother Percival, shook hands with her heartily in the eyes of his guests before he said a word of welcome to them; and one of those guests, a remarkably broad woman, with a red face, a wide snub nose, and a front of light flaxen hair, who had stepped into the house leaning on the earl's arm—having, in fact, seized upon it unasked, and seemed to be assuming a great deal of authority—turned short round to stare at Mirrable, and screwed her little light eyes together, to take a better view.

"Who is she, Hartledon? Who is she?"

"Mrs. Mirrable," answered his lordship rather shortly. "I think you must have seen her before. She has been Hartledon's mistress since my mother died," he rather pointedly added, for he saw incipient defiance of Mirrable in the old lady's countenance.

"O, Hartledon's upper servant, I presume," cried the old lady, as majestically as her squeaking harsh voice allowed her to speak. "Perhaps you'll tell her who I am, Hartledon; and that I have promised to undertake to preside here for a little while."

"I believe Mrs. Mirrable knows you, ma'am," spoke up Percival Elster, for Lord Hartledon had turned away, and was lost amidst his guests. "You have seen the Countess Dowager of Kirton, have you not, Mirrable?"

The Countess Dowager faced round upon

the speaker, her voice and her face alike sharp.

"O, it's *you*, is it, Val Elster! Who asked you to interfere? I'll see the rooms, Mirrable, and the different arrangements you have made. Maude, where are you? Come with me."

A tall stately girl, with handsome features, raven-dark hair and eyes, and a brilliant colour, extricated herself from the crowd. It was the Lady Maude Kirton. Mirrable went first; the Countess Dowager followed, talking fast and volubly; and Maude brought up the rear. Other servants came forward to see after the rest of the guests.

The most remarkable quality observable in the Countess Dowager, apart from her great breadth, was her restlessness. She seemed never still; her legs had a fidgety, nervous movement in them, and in moments of excitement, which were not unfrequent, she was given to execute a sort of war-dance. Old she was not; but her peculiar graces of person, her rotund form, her badly-made front of flat flaxen curls, which was rarely in its place, made her appear so. A bold, scheming, unscrupulous, vulgar-minded woman, who had never been considerate of other people's feelings in her life, whether they might be her equals or her inferiors. In her day she must have been rather tall—nearly as tall as that elegant Maude, who followed her; but her astounding width caused her now to appear short. She went looking into the different rooms, as shown to her by Mirrable, and pitched upon the best for herself and daughter.

"Three en suite. Yes, that will be the thing, Mirrable. Lady Maude Kirton will take the inner one, and I'll occupy this, and my maid the outer one. Very good. Now you may order the luggage up."

"But, my lady," objected Mirrable, "these are the best rooms in the house,—all large; and each has a separate entrance, as you perceive. With so many guests to provide for, your maid cannot take up one of these rooms."

"What's that?" cried the Countess Dowager. "My maid not take up one of these rooms? You insolent woman! Do you know that I am come here with my nephew, Lord Hartledon, to be the sole mistress of his house, and of every body in it. You'd better mind *your* behaviour, for I can tell you that I shall look pretty sharp after it."

"Then," said Mirrable, who never allowed herself to be put out by any earthly thing, and rarely argued against the stream, "as your ladyship has come here as sole mistress, perhaps you will apportion out the rooms to the guests."

"Let them portion them out for themselves," cried the Countess Dowager. "These three are mine; others may scramble as they can. It's Hartledon's fault. I told him not to invite a heap. You and I shall get on together very well, I've no doubt, Mirrable," she continued, in a false, fawning voice; for she was remarkably alive at all times to her own interests. "Am I to understand that you are the housekeeper?"

"I am acting as the housekeeper at present," was Mirrable's answer. "When my lord went to town, after my lady's death, the housekeeper went also, and has remained there. Lord Elster—Lord

Hartledon, I mean—the other name comes more familiar—has not lived yet at Hartledon, and we have had no establishment."

"Then who are you?"

"I was maid to Lady Hartledon for many years. Her ladyship treated me more as a friend at last; and the young gentlemen always did so."

"*Very* good," cried the untrue voice. "And now, Mirrable, you can go down and send up some tea for myself and Lady Maude. What time do we dine?"

"Mr. Elster ordered it for eight o'clock to-night."

"And what business had *he* to take orders upon himself?" and the little pale eyes flashed with anger. "Who's Val Elster, that he should interfere? I sent word by the servants we'd not dine till nine."

"Mr. Elster is in his own house, madam; he—"

"In his own house!" shrieked Lady Kirton. "It's no house of his; it's his brother's. And I wish I was his brother for a day only; *I'*d let Mr.

Val know what presumption comes to. Can't the dinner be put back?"

"I'm afraid not, my lady."

"Ugh!" snapped the Countess Dowager. "Send up the tea at once, Mirrable; and let it be strong, mind, with its full share of green. And some delicate slices of rolled bread-and-butter, and a few thin sippets of toast, well buttered."

Mirrable departed with the commands, more inclined to laugh at the selfish old woman than to be angry. She remembered the Countess Dowager arriving on an unexpected visit some three or four years before, and finding the Earl of Hartledon away, and the Countess ill in bed. She remained three days, completely upsetting the house; so completely upsetting the sick Lady Hartledon, that the latter was glad to lend her a sum of money and get rid of her. Truth to say, Lady Kirton had never been a welcome guest at Hartledon; had been shunned, in fact, and kept away by all sorts of strategy. The only other visit she had paid the family, in Mirrable's remembrance, was to the town-house, when the children were young.

Poor little Val had been taught by his nurse to look upon her as a "bogy:" he went about in real terror of her; and her ladyship detected the feeling, and administered sly, cruel pinches whenever they met. Perhaps neither of them had completely overcome the antagonism from that time to this.

A scrambling sort of life had been Lady Kirton's. The wife of a very poor and improvident Irish peer, who had died early, leaving her badly provided for, her days had been one long scramble *to live*—to live and avoid creditors. Now in Ireland, now on the Continent, now coming out for a few brief weeks of fashion, and now on the wing to some place of safety, had she dodged about, and become utterly unscrupulous. There was a whole troop of children, more than could be counted, who had been let go to the good or the bad very much in their own fashion, with but little help or hindrance from their mother. All the daughters were married now, except Maude, mostly to German barons and French counts. One had espoused a marquis—natal country not clearly indicated; one

an Italian duke: but the marquis lived somewhere
over in Algeria up a two-pair story, and the duke
condescended to sing an occasional song on the
Italian stage. It was all one to Lady Kirton.
They had taken their own way, and she washed
her hands of them as easily as if they had never
belonged to her. Had they been able to supply
her with a bank-note on a pinch, or to welcome
her on a protracted visit, they had been her well-
beloved and most estimable daughters. Of the
younger sons, all were dispersed; the Dowager
neither knew nor cared where. Now and again a
piteous begging-letter would come to her from one
or the other of them, which she railed at and
scolded over, and bade Maude answer. Her eldest
son, the earl, had married some four or five years
ago, and the Countess Dowager's lines had been
harder since. Before that event she could go to
the place in Ireland whenever she liked (circumstances permitting), and stay as long as she liked;
but that was over now. For the young countess,
who on her own score spent all the money her
husband could scrape together, and more, had

taken an inveterate dislike to her mother-in-law, and would not tolerate her.

Never, since she was thus thrown upon her own resources, had the Countess Dowager's lucky star been in the ascendant as it had been this season, for she contrived to fasten herself upon the young Lord Hartledon, and secure a firm footing in his town-house. She called him her nephew, —" My nephew Hartledon;" but that was a little improvement upon the actual relationship, for she and the late Lady Hartledon had been cousins only. She invited herself for a week's sojourn in May, and had never gone away again; and it was now August. She had come down with him, sans cérémonie, to Hartledon; had told him (making a great favour of it) that she would look after his house and his guests during her stay, as his mother would have done. Easy, careless, good-natured, the earl acquiesced, and took it all as a matter of course. She was ever all bland suavity to *him*.

None knew better on which side her bread was buttered than the Countess Dowager. She liked it buttered on both, and generally contrived to get it.

She had come down to Hartledon House with one fixed determination—that she did not quit it until the Lady Maude was its mistress. For a long while Maude had been her sole hope. Her other daughters had married according to their fancy—and what had come of it?—but Maude was different. Maude had her great beauty; and Maude, truth to say, was nearly as selfishly alive to her own interest as her mother. *She* should marry well, and so be in a position to afford a shelter to the poor, homeless, wandering Dowager. Had she taken the pick of the whole batch of peers, not one could have been found more eligible than he whom fortune seemed to have turned up on purpose—the Earl of Hartledon; and before the Countess Dowager had been one week his guest in London she began her scheming. Lady Maude was nothing loth. Young, beautiful, vain, selfish, she yet possessed a woman's susceptible heart; though suddenly surrounded with luxury, dress, pomp, show, which are said to deaden the feelings, and which in some measure do deaden them, Lady Maude insensibly managed to fall in love, as deeply as ever did an obscure damsel of romance. She had met him first two years before, when he was Viscount Elster; had liked him then. Their relationship sanctioned their being now much together, and the Lady Maude lost her heart to him.

Would it bring forth fruit, this scheming of the Countess Dowager's, and Maude's own love? In her wildest hopes the old woman never dreamt of what that fruit would be; or, unscrupulous as she was by habit, unfeeling by nature, she might have carried away Maude from Hartledon before they had well set foot in it.

Of the three parties more immediately concerned, the only innocent one—innocent of any intentions—was Lord Hartledon. He liked Maude very well as a cousin, but else he did not care for her. They might succeed—at least, had circumstances gone on well, without the miserable interruption that came, they might have succeeded —in winning him at last; but it would not have been from ardent love. His present feeling towards Maude was one of indifference; and of marriage at all he had not begun to think. Val

Elster, on the contrary, regarded Maude with warm admiration. Her beauty had charms for him, and he had been oftener at her side but for the watchful Countess Dowager. It would have been a horrible thing had Maude fallen in love with the wrong brother, and the old lady grew to hate him for the fear, as well as on her own score. The feeling of dislike, begun in Val's childhood, had ripened in the last month or two to almost open hatred. He was always in the way. Many a time when Lord Hartledon might have enjoyed a tête-à-tête with Maude, Val Elster was there to spoil it. But the culminating point had arrived one day, when Val, half laughingly, half seriously, told the Dowager, who had been provoking him almost beyond bearing, that she might spare her pains in regard to Maude, for Hartledon would never bite. But that he took his pleasant face beyond her reach, it might have suffered, for her fingers were held out alarmingly. From that time she took another private scheme upon her hands— that of getting Percival Elster out of his brother's favour and his brother's house. Val, on his part, seriously advised his brother *not* to allow the Kirtons to come to Hartledon; and this reached the ears of the Dowager. You may be sure it did not tend to soothe her. Lord Hartledon only laughed at Val, saying they might come if they liked: what did it matter? But, strange to say, Val Elster was as a very reed in the hands of the old woman. Let her once get hold of him, and she could turn him any way she pleased: he felt afraid of her, he bent to her will. The feeling may have had its rise partly in the strange fear of her imbued into his boyhood, and partly in the yieldingness of his natural disposition. However that might be, it was a fact; and Val could no more have openly opposed the resolute, sharp-tongued old woman to her face than he could have changed his nature. He rarely called her any thing but "ma'am," as their nurse had taught him and his brothers and sisters to do in those long-past years.

Before eight o'clock the guests had all assembled in the drawing-room, except the Countess Dowager and Maude. Lord Hartledon was going about amidst them, talking to one and another of the beauties of this, his late father's, place; hardly yet thought of as his own. He was a tall slender man; in figure very much resembling Percival, but not in face: the one was dark, the other light. There was also the same indolent sort of movement, a certain languor of air discernible in both; proclaiming the undoubted fact, that both were idle of disposition and given to ennui. There the resemblance ended. Lord Hartledon had nothing of the irresolution of Mr. Elster, but was sufficiently decisive in character, prompt in action.

A noble room, this that they were in, as many of the rooms were in the fine old mansion. Lord Hartledon opened the inner door, and took them into another, to show them the portrait of his brother George—a fine young man also, with a fair, pleasing countenance.

"He is like Elster; he's not like you, Hartledon," cried out a young man, whose name was Carteret.

"*Was*, you mean, Carteret," corrected Lord Hartledon, his tone one of sad regret. "There was a great family resemblance between us all, I believe."

"He died from an accident, did he not?" said Mr. O'Moore, an Irishman, who liked to be called "The O'Moore."

"Yes."

Percival Elster turned to his brother, and spoke in a low tone, "I say, Edward, was any particular person suspected of having fired the shot?"

"None. A set of loose, lawless characters were out that night, and—"

"What in the world are you looking at here?"

The interruption came from Lady Kirton, who was sailing into the room with Maude. A striking contrast the one presented to the other. Maude in pink silk and a pink wreath, her haughty face raised in pride, her dark eyes flashing radiantly beautiful. The old Dowager, as broad as she was high, her face rouged, her snub nose short and always carried in the air, her light eyes unmeaning, her flaxen eyebrows thick, her flaxen curls surmounted by a high pea-green turban. Her choice attire was generally composed, as to-day, of some cheap, flimsy, gauzy material of a bright hue. This evening it was orange colour, all flounces and frills, with a scarf or mantle of lace; and she generally had innumerable ends of quilted net flying about her skirts, not unlike tails. It was certain she did not spend much money upon her own attire; and how she procured the rich dresses for Maude that the latter appeared in, was ever a mystery. You can hardly fancy the bedecked old figure that she made. The O'Moore nearly laughed out, as he civilly turned to answer her question.

"We were looking at this portrait, Lady Kirton."

"And saying how much he was like Val," put in young Carteret, between whom and the Dowager there was also existing warfare. "Val, which was the elder of you?"

"George was."

"Then his death made you presumptive

heir," cried the thoughtless young man, speaking upon impulse.

"Presumptive heir to what?" asked the Dowager, snapping at the words.

"To Hartledon."

"*He* heir to Hartledon! He, Val Elster! Don't you trouble yourself, young man, that Val Elster's ever likely to come into Hartledon. Do you want to shoot his lordship, as *he* was shot?"

The uncalled-for retort, the strangely intemperate tone, the quick passionate fling of the hand towards the portrait at the emphasised word "*he*," astonished young Carteret not a little. Others were surprised also; and not one present but stared at the speaker. But she said no more. The pea-green turban and the flaxen curls were nodding ominously; and that was all.

The animus to Val Elster was very marked. Lord Hartledon glanced at his brother with a smile, and led the way back to the other drawing-room. At that moment the butler announced dinner; the party filed across the hall to the fine old dining-room, and began finding their seats.

"I shall sit there, Val Elster. You can take a chair on the side."

Val did look surprised at this. He was about to take the foot of his brother's table, as usual; and there was the pea-green turban standing over him, waiting to usurp it. It would have been quite beyond Val Elster, in his ultra-sensitiveness, to tell her she should not have it; but he did feel annoyed. He was sweet-tempered, however. Moreover, he was a gentleman, and he only waited to make one remark.

"I fear you will not like this place, ma'am. Won't it look odd to see a lady at the bottom of the table?"

"I have promised my dear nephew to act as the house's mistress, and to see after his guests; and I don't choose to sit on the side under those circumstances." But she had looked at Lord Hartledon for a full minute, and hesitated before she spoke. Perhaps she thought his lordship would resign the head of the table to her, and take the foot himself! If so, she was mistaken.

"You will be more comfortable on the side, Lady Kirton," cried out the earl, when he could discover what the bustle was about.

"Not at all; not at all, Hartledon."

"But I like my brother to face me, ma'am. It is his accustomed place."

Remonstrance was useless. The Dowager nodded her pea-green turban, and firmly seated herself. Val Elster dexterously found a seat next Lady Maude; and a gay gleam of triumph shot out of his deep-blue eyes as he glanced at the Dowager. It was not the seat she would have wished him to take; but to interfere again might have imperilled her own place. Maude laughed. She did not care for Val—rather despised him indeed in her heart; but he was the most attractive man present, and she liked to be admired by such.

Another link in the chain! For how many,

many days and years, dating from that evening, did that awful old woman take a seat, with intervals, at the Earl of Hartledon's table, and assume it as a right!

CHAPTER V.

A RISING JEALOUSY.

A WET day in the country, especially in August, is not pleasant. The rain came pouring down on the Monday morning; and Lord Hartledon stood at the window of the Countess Dowager's private sitting-room — one she had unceremoniously adopted for her own use — smoking a cigar, and watching the clouds. Any cigar but his would have been consigned to the other side the door. Mr. Elster had only shown (by mere accident) the tail of his cigar-case, and the Dowager immediately demanded what he meant by displaying that article in the presence of ladies. A few minutes afterwards Lord Hartledon entered, smoking one, and was allowed to enjoy it with impunity. Good-tempered Val's delicate lips broke into a silent smile as he marked the contrast.

He lounged on the sofa, doing nothing, in

his idle fashion; Lord Hartledon watched the clouds, and watched again. On the previous Saturday night the gentlemen had entered into an argument touching boating: the result was, that a match on the river was arranged, and some bets were pending on it. It had been fixed to come off this day, Monday; but if the rain continued to come down, it must be postponed; for the ladies, who had been promised the treat, would not venture out to see it.

"It's come on purpose, I know," grumbled the earl. "Yesterday was as fine and bright a day as could be, the glass standing at set fair; and now, just because this boating was to come off, the rain peppers down!"

It was a fair scene, barring the rain, that he looked out upon. The room faced the back of the house, and, beyond the lovely grounds, green slopes extended to the river, tolerably wide here, and winding past so peacefully in its course. The distant landscape, as seen from these windows, was beautiful—almost like a scene in fairyland.

The restless Dowager—in a nondescript head-dress this morning, with a tuft of red feathers in it sticking up straight, and voluminous skirts of brown net, a jacket and flounces to match—betook herself to the side of the earl.

"Where d'ye get the boats?" she asked.

"O, they are kept lower down, at the boat-house," he replied, puffing at the cigar. "You can't see it from here; it's beyond Dr. Ashton's; lots of 'em; all sorts; to be had for the hiring. O, talking of Dr. Ashton, they will dine here to-day, ma'am."

"Who will?" asked Lady Kirton.

"The doctor, Mrs. Ashton (if she's well enough), and Miss Ashton."

"Who are they, my dear nephew?"

"Why, don't you know? Dr. Ashton preached to you yesterday. He is the rector of Calne: you must have heard of Dr. Ashton. They will be calling this morning, I expect."

"And you have invited them to dinner! Well, there'll be room. One must do the civil on occasion to this sort of people."

The young nobleman burst into a laugh. "You'll not say 'this sort of people' when you see the Ashtons, Lady Kirton. They stand as high as we do. Dr. Ashton has refused a bishopric, and Anne is the sweetest girl ever created."

Lady Maude, who was drawing, and exchanging a desultory sentence once in a way with Val, looked up suddenly. Her colour had heightened, though it was brilliant at all times.

"Are you speaking of my maid?" she said—and it might be that she had not attended to the conversation, and asked in ignorance, not in scorn. "Her name is Anne."

"I was speaking of Anne Ashton," said the earl.

"Allow me to beg Anne Ashton's pardon," returned Lady Maude; her tone this time one of unmistakable mockery. "Anne is so common a name amidst servants."

"I don't care whether it is common amidst servants or uncommon," spoke Lord Hartledon rather hotly, as if he would resent the covert sneer: "it is Anne Ashton's; and I love the name for her sake. But I think it a pretty name; and should, if she did not bear it; prettier than yours, Maude."

"And pray who *is* Anne Ashton?" demanded the Countess Dowager, with as much hauteur as so queer an old figure and face could put on, while the Lady Maude bent over her employment with white lips.

"She is Dr. Ashton's daughter," spoke the earl, shortly. "My father valued him above all men. He loved Anne too—loved her dearly; and—though I don't know whether it is quite fair to Anne to let this out—the probable future connection between the families was most welcome to him. Next to my father, we boys reverenced the doctor; he was our tutor, in a sort, when we were staying at Hartledon; at least to poor George and Val: they used to read with him."

"And you would hint at some alliance between you and this Anne Ashton!" cried the Countess Dowager in a hot fume; for she thought she saw a fear that the great prize might slip through her fingers. "What sort of an alliance, I'd like to ask? Be careful what you say, Hartledon; you may injure the young woman."

"I'll take care I don't injure Anne Ashton," returned the earl, enjoying her temper. "As to an alliance with her—my earnest wish is, as it was my father's, that time may bring it about. Val there knows I do."

Val glanced at his brother by way of answer. He had taken no part in the discussion; his slight lips were drawn down, as he balanced a pair of scissors on his forefinger, and he looked less good-tempered than usual.

"Has she red hair and sky-blue eyes and a doll's face? Does she sit in the pew under the reading-desk with three other dolls?" asked the foaming Dowager.

Lord Hartledon turned round and stared at the speaker in wonder—*what* was it that was exciting her?

"She has soft brown hair and eyes, and a sweet gentle face; she is a graceful, elegant, attractive girl," said the earl curtly. "She sat alone yesterday; for Arthur was in another part of the church, and Mrs. Ashton was not there. Mrs. Ashton is not in good health, she tells me, and cannot always come. The rector's pew is the one with green curtains."

"O, *that* vulgar-looking girl!" exclaimed Lady Maude, her unjust words—and she knew they were unjust—trembling on her lips. "The Grand Sultan might exalt her to be his chief wife, but he could never make a lady of her, or get her to look like one."

"Be quiet, Maude," cried the Countess Dowager, who, with all her own mistakes, had the sense to see that this sort of disparagement would but recoil with interest, and who did not like the expression of Lord Hartledon's face. "You talk as if you had seen this Mrs. Ashton, Hartledon, since your return."

"I should not be many hours at Hartledon without seeing Mrs. Ashton," he answered. "That's where I was yesterday afternoon, ma'am, when you were so kindly anxious in your inquiries as to what had become of me. I daresay I was absent an unconscionable time. I never know how it passes, once I am with Anne."

"We represent Love as blind, you know," spoke Maude, in her desperation, unable to steady her pallid lips. "You apparently do not see it, Lord Hartledon, but the young woman is the very essence of vulgarity."

A pause followed the speech. The Countess Dowager turned towards her daughter in a blazing rage, and Val Elster quitted the room.

"Maude," said the earl, "I am sorry to tell you that you have put your foot in it."

"Thank you," panted Lady Maude, in her agitation. "For giving my opinion of your Anne Ashton?"

"Precisely. You have driven Val away in suppressed indignation."

"Is Val of the Anne Ashton faction, that the truth should tell upon him, as well as upon you?" she returned, striving to maintain an assumption of sarcastic coldness.

"It is upon him that the words will tell. Anne is engaged to him."

"Is it true? Is Val really engaged to her?" cried the Countess Dowager in an ecstasy of relief, lifting up her snub nose and her blooming cheeks, while the glad light came into Maude's eyes again. "I did hear he was engaged to some lady; but such reports of younger sons go for nothing."

"Val was engaged to her before he went abroad. Whether he will get her or not, is another thing."

"To hear you talk, Hartledon, one might have supposed you cared for the girl yourself," cried Lady Kirton; but her brow was smooth again, and her tone soft as honey. "You should be more cautious."

"Cautious! Why so? I love and respect Anne beyond any girl on earth. But that Val hastened to make hay when the sun shone, while I fell asleep under the hedge, I don't know but I might have tried for her myself," he added, with a laugh. "However, it shall not be my fault if Val does not get her."

The Countess Dowager said no more. She was worldly-wise in her way, and thought it best to leave well alone. She sailed out of the room—nose up—leaving them alone together: it was what she was fond of doing.

"Is it not rather—rather beneath an Elster to marry an obscure country clergyman's daughter?" began Lady Maude to his lordship, a strange bitterness filling her heart.

"I tell you, Maude, the Ashtons are equal to ourselves. He is a proud old doctor of divinity—not old, however—of irreproachable family and of large private fortune."

"You spoke of him as a tutor?"

"A tutor! O, I said he was in a measure our tutor when we were young. I meant in training us—in training us to good; and he allowed George and Val to read with him, and directed their studies: all for love, and out of the friendship he and my father bore each other. Dr. Ashton a paid tutor!" ejaculated his lordship, laughing at the notion. "Dr. Ashton an obscure country clergyman! And even if he were, who is Val, that he should set himself up?"

"He is Val Elster, the Honourable."

"Very honourable! Val is an unlucky dog of a spend-all; that's what Val is. See how many times he has been set up on his legs!—and has always come down again. He had that place in the Government that my father got him. He had the attachéship in Paris; he had the subsequent one at Vienna—O, ever so many good chances he has had, and he drops through all. One can't help loving Val; he is an attractive, sweet-tempered, good-natured fellow; but he was certainly born under an unlucky star. Elster's Folly!"

"Val will drop through more chances yet," remarked Lady Maude. "I pity Miss Ashton, if she means waiting for him."

"Means it! She loves him passionately—devotedly. She would wait for him all her life, and think it happiness only to see him once in a way."

"As an astronomer looks at a star through a telescope," laughed Lady Maude; "and Val is not worth the devotion."

"Val is not a bad fellow in the main; quite the contrary, Maude. Of course we all know his besetting sin—irresolution. A child might sway him, either for good or for ill. The very best thing that could happen to Val would be his marriage with Anne. She is sensible, judicious, loving; and I think Val could not fail to keep straight under her influence. If Dr. Ashton could but be brought to see the matter in this light!"

"Can he not?"

"He thinks — and I don't say he has not reason—that Val should show some proof of stability before his marriage, instead of waiting until after it. The doctor has not gone the length of parting them, or of suspending the engagement; but he is prepared to be strict and exacting as to Mr. Val's line of conduct; and I fancy the suspicion that it would be so has kept Val away from Calne."

"What will be done?"

"I hardly know. Val does not make a confidant of me, and I can't get to the bottom of how he is situated. Debts I am sure he has; but whether——"

"Val always had plenty of those," interrupted Maude.

"True. When my father died, three parts of Val's inheritance went to pay off debts nobody knew he had contracted. The worst is, he glides into these difficulties unwittingly, led and swayed by others. We don't say Elster's sin, or Elster's crimes; we say Elster's folly. I don't believe Val ever in his life did a bad thing of deliberate intention. Designing people get hold of him—fast fellows who are going down hill headlong themselves—and Val, unable to say No, is drawn here and drawn there, and tumbles with them into a quagmire, and perhaps has to pay his friends' costs, as well as his own, before he can get out of it. Do you believe in luck, Maude?"

"In luck?" answered Maude, raising her eyes at the abruptly-put question. "I don't know."

"I believe in it. I believe that some are born under a lucky star, and others under an unlucky one. Val is one of the latter. He is always unlucky. Set him up, and down he comes again. I don't think I ever knew Val lucky in my life. Look at his nearly blowing his arm off that time in Scotland! You will laugh at me, I daresay, Maude; but a thought crosses me at odd moments that his ill-luck will prevail still, in the matter of Miss Ashton. Not if I can help it, however; I'll do my best for Anne's sake."

"You seem to think very much of her yourself," cried Lady Maude, her cheeks crimsoning with an angry flush.

"I do—as Val's future wife. I love Anne Ashton better than any one in the world. We all loved her. So would you if you knew her. In my mother's last illness Anne was a greater comfort to her than Laura was."

"Should you ever think of a wife on your own score, she may not like this warm praise of Miss Anne Ashton," said Lady Maude, assiduously drawing, her hot face bent down to within an inch of the cardboard.

"Not like it? She'd not be such an idiot, I hope, as to dislike it. Is not Anne going to be my brother's wife? Did you suppose I spoke of

Anne in that way?—you must have been dreaming, Maude."

Lady Maude hoped she had been. The young nobleman took his cigar from his mouth, ran a penknife through its end, and began smoking again.

"That time is far enough off, Maude. *I* am not going to tie myself up with a wife, or to think of one either, for many a long year to come."

Her heart beat with a painful throbbing. "Why not?"

"No danger. My wild oats are not sown yet, any more than Val's; only you don't hear tell of them, because I have money to back me, and he has not. I must find a girl I'd like to make my wife, before that event comes off, Maude; and I have not found her yet."

Lady Maude damaged her landscape. She sketched a tree where a chimney ought to have been, and laid the fault upon her pencil.

"It has been real sport, Maude, ever since I came home from knocking about abroad, to hear and see the old ladies. They think Edward, Earl of Hartledon, is to be caught with a bait; and

that bait is each one's own enchanting daughter.
Let them angle, an' they please—what does it
hurt? They are amused, and I am none the
worse. I enjoy a laugh sometimes, while I take
care of myself; as I have need to do, or I might
find myself the victim of some detestable breach-of-
promise affair, and have to stand damages. But
for Anne Ashton, Val would have had his head in
that Westminster-noose a score of times; and the
wonder is that he has kept out of it. No, thank
you, my ladies; I am not a marrying man."

"Why do you tell me this?" asked Lady
Maude, a sick faintness stealing alike over her
face and her heart.

"Do you not care to hear it? You are one of
ourselves, and I tell you any thing. It will be fun
for you, Maude, if you'll open your eyes and look
on. There are some in the house now who—"
He stopped and laughed.

"I'd rather not hear this!" she cried out passionately. "Don't tell it me."

The earl looked at her, begged her pardon, and
quitted the room with his cigar. Lady Maude,

black as night, dashed her pencil on the cardboard, and scored her pretty sketch all over with ugly black lines. Her face looked ugly then.

"Why did he say it to me?" she asked of her burning heart. "Was it said with a purpose? Has he found out that I *love* him? and that my shallow old mother is one of the subtlest of the anglers? and that——"

"What on earth are you at with your drawing, Maude?"

"O, I have grown sick of the piece. I am not in a drawing mood to-day, mamma."

"And how fierce you were looking," pursued the Countess Dowager, who had darted in at rather an inopportune moment for Maude—darting in on people at such moments being her custom. "And that was the sketch Hartledon got you to do for him from the old painting!"

"He may do it himself, if he wants it done."

"Where is Hartledon?"

"I don't know. Gone out somewhere."

"Has he offended you, or vexed you? Speak out."

"Well, he did vex me. He has just been assuring me with the coolest air that he should never marry; or, at least, not for years and years. He told me to notice what a heap of girls were after him—or their mothers for them—and the fun he had over it, he not a marrying man!"

"Is that all? You need not have put yourself in a fantigue, and spoilt your drawing. Lord Hartledon shall be your husband, Maude, before six months are over—or reproach me ever afterwards with being a false prophetess and a bungling manager."

Maude's brow cleared. She had almost childlike confidence in the tact of her unscrupulous mother.

But how the morning's conversation altogether rankled in her heart, none, save herself, could tell; ay, and in that of the Dowager. Although Anne Ashton was the betrothed of Percival Elster, and Lord Hartledon's freely-avowed love for her was evidently that of a brother, and he had said he should do all he could to promote the marriage, jealousy of the strongest nature had taken possession of Lady Maude's heart. She already hated Anne Ashton with a fierce and bitter hatred; she turned sick with envy when, in the morning visit that was that day paid by the Ashtons, she saw that Anne was really what Lord Hartledon had described her,—one of the sweetest, most lovable, most charming of girls; almost without a compeer in the world for grace and goodness and beauty. She turned more sick with envy when at the dinner afterwards, to which the Ashtons came, Lord Hartledon devoted himself to them, almost to the neglecting of his other guests, lingering much with Anne. The Countess Dowager marked it also, and was furious. Nothing could be urged against them; they were unexceptionable. The doctor, a chatty, straightforward, energetic man, of eminent intellect and learning, and emphatically a gentleman; his wife attracting by her unobtrusive gentleness; his daughter by her sweet grace, her modest self-possession. Whatever Maude Kirton might do, she could never, for very shame, attempt to disparage them again. Surely there was no just reason for the hatred which took possession of Maude's heart; a hatred that could never be plucked out again.

But Maude knew how to dissemble. It pleased her to affect a sudden and violent fancy, a friendship for Anne.

"Hartledon told me how much I should like you," she whispered, as they sat together on a sofa after dinner, to which Maude had drawn her. "He said I should find you the dearest girl I ever met; and I do so. May I call you 'Anne'?"

Not for a moment did Miss Ashton answer. Truth to say, far from reciprocating the sudden fancy boasted of by Maude, she had taken an unaccountable dislike to her. Something of falsity in the tone, of sudden hardiesse in the handsome black eyes, acted upon Anne as an instinctive warning.

"As you please, Lady Maude."

"Thank you so much. Hartledon whispered to me the secret about you and Val—Percival, I mean. Shall you accomplish the task, think you?"

"What task?"

"That of turning him from his evil ways."

"His evil ways?" repeated Anne, in a surprised indignation she did not care to check. "I do not understand you, Lady Maude."

"Pardon me, my dear Anne: it was hazardous so to speak *to you*. I ought to have said his thoughtless ways. Quant à moi, je ne vois pas la différence. Do you understand French?"

Miss Ashton looked at her, really not seeing what this style of conversation might mean. Maude continued; she had the habit of putting forth a sting on occasion, or what she hoped might be a sting.

"You are staring at the superfluous question. Of course it was one in these *French* days, when every body learns it. What was I saying? O, about Percival. Should he ever get the luck to marry, meaning the income, he will make a docile husband; but his wife will have to keep him under her finger and thumb; she must be master as well as mistress, for his own sake."

"I think Mr. Elster would not care to be thus

spoken of," said Miss Ashton, her face beginning to glow.

"You devoted girl! It is you who don't care to hear it. Take care, Anne: too much love is not good for gaining the mastership; and I have heard that you are—shall I say it?—folle de lui."

Anne, in spite of her calm good sense, was actually provoked to a retort in kind, and felt terribly vexed with herself for it afterwards. "A rumour of the same sort has been breathed as to the Lady Maude Kirton's regard for Lord Hartledon."

"Has it?" returned Lady Maude, with a cool tone and a glowing face. "You are angry with me without cause. Have I not offered to swear to you an eternal friendship?"

Anne shook her head, and her lips parted with a curious expression. "I do not swear so lightly, Lady Maude."

"What if I were to avow to you that it is true?—that I do love Lord Hartledon, deeply as it is known you love his brother," she added, dropping her voice,—"would you believe me?"

Anne looked at the speaker's face, but could read nothing. Was she in jest or earnest?

"No, I would not believe you," she said with a smile. "If you did love him, you would not proclaim it."

"Exactly. I was jesting. What is Lord Hartledon to me?—save that we are cousins, and passably good friends. I must avow one thing, that I like him better than I do his brother."

"For that, no avowal is necessary, Lady Maude; it is a sufficiently evident fact."

"You are right, Anne," Maude replied; and for once she spoke earnestly. "I do *not* like Percival Elster. But I will always be civil to him for your sweet sake."

"Why do you dislike him?—if I may ask it. Have you any particular reason?"

"I have no reason in the world. He is a good-natured, gentlemanly fellow; and I know no ill of him, except that he is always getting into scrapes, and dropping, as I hear, a lot of money. But if he got out of his last guinea, and went in holes to his coats, it would be nothing to me, that

I need dislike him; so *that's* not it. One does take antipathies; I daresay you do, Miss Ashton. What a blessing Lord Hartledon did not die in that fever he caught last year! Val would have inherited. What a mercy!"

"That he lived? or that Val is not the earl?"

"Both. But I believe I meant that Val is not the earl."

"You think he would not have made a worthy inheritor?"

"A worthy inheritor? O, I was not glancing at that phase of the question. Here he comes! I will give up my seat to him."

It is possible Lady Maude expected some pretty phrases of affectation; begging her not to, begging her to keep it. If so, she was mistaken. Anne Ashton was one of those essentially quiet, self-possessed girls in society, whose manners seem almost to border on apathy. She did not say "Do go," or "Don't go." She was entirely passive; and Maude moved away half ashamed of herself, and feeling, in spite of her jealousy and her prejudice, that if ever there was a lady-like girl upon earth, it was Anne Ashton.

"How do you like her, Anne?" asked Val Elster, dropping into the vacant place.

"Not much."

"Don't you? She is very handsome."

"Very handsome indeed. Quite beautiful. But still I don't like her."

"You would like her if you knew her. She has a rare spirit; only the old Dowager keeps it down."

"I don't think she much likes you, Val."

"She is welcome to dislike me," returned Val Elster.

CHAPTER VI.

AN ENCOUNTER AT THE BRIDGE.

THE famous boat-race was postponed. Some of the competitors had discovered they should be the better for a few days' training, and the contest was fixed for the following Monday.

Not a day of the intervening week but sundry pretty little cockle-shells,—things that the ladies had already begun to designate as the "wager-boats," each containing a gentleman occupant, exercising his arms on a pair of sculls,—might be seen any hour passing and repassing on the water; and the green slopes of Hartledon, which here formed the bank of the river, grew to be tenanted with fair occupants. Of course they had their favourites, these ladies, and their little bets of gloves on them.

As the day for the contest drew on, the interest became really exciting; and on the Saturday morning there was quite a crowd on the banks. The whole week, since the Monday, had been most beautiful—calm, warm, charmingly lovely. Percival Elster, in his rather idle fashion, was not going out to the contest: there were enough without him, he said.

He was standing now, talking to Anne. His face wore a sad expression, as she glanced up at him from beneath the sheltering white feather of her rather large-brimmed straw hat. Anne had been a great deal at Hartledon that week, and was as eager for the race as any of them, wearing Lord Hartledon's colours.

"How did you hear it, Anne?" he was asking.

"Mamma told me. She came into my room when I was putting on my hat just now, and said there had been words."

"Well, it's true. The doctor took me to task exactly as he used to when I was a boy. He said my course of life was sinful; and I rather fired at that. Idle and useless it may be, but sinful it is not: and I said so. He explained that he meant that, and persisted in his assertion—that an idle, aimless, profitless life was a sinful one. Do you know the rest?"

"No," she faltered.

"He said he would give me to the end of the year. And if I were then still pursuing my present frittering course of life, doing no good for myself or for any body else—those were the words, 'doing no good for myself or for any body else'—he should cancel the engagement. Anne, my darling, I see how this pains you."

She was suppressing her tears with difficulty. "Papa will be sure to keep his word, Percival. He is so resolute when he thinks he is right."

"The worst is, it's gospel truth. I do fall into all sorts of scrapes, and I have got out of money, and I do fritter my time away," acknowledged the young man in his candour. "And all the while, Anne, I am thinking and hoping to do right. If ever I get set on my legs again, *won't* I keep on them!"

"But how many times have you said so before!" she whispered.

"Half the follies for which I am now paying were committed when I was but a boy," he said. "One of the men now visiting here, Dawkes, got me to put my name to a bill for him for fifteen hundred pounds, and I had to pay it. It hampered me for years; and in the end I know I must have paid it twice over. I might have pleaded that I was under age when he got my signature, but it would not have been honourable."

"And you never profited by the transaction?"

"Never by a sixpence. It was done for Dawkes's accommodation, not mine. He ought to have paid it, you say? My dear, he is a man of straw, and never had fifteen hundred pounds of his own in his life."

"Does Lord Hartledon know of this? I wonder he has him here."

"I did not tell of it at the time; and the thing's past and done with now. I only mention it to give you an idea of what the nature of my embarrassments and scrapes has been. Not one in ten has really been incurred for myself: they only fall upon me. One must buy experience."

Terribly vexed was that sweet face, an almost painful sadness pervading the generally sunny features.

"I will never give you up, Anne," he continued, with emotion. "I told the doctor so. I'd rather give up life. And you know that your love is mine."

"But my duty is theirs. And if it came to a contest—O Percival! you know, you know which would have to give place. Papa is so resolute in right."

"It's a shame that fortune should be so unequally divided!" cried the young man, in explosive resentment. "Here's Edward with an income of thirty thousand pounds, and I, his own brother, but a year or two younger, can't boast of a fourth part as many hundreds!"

"O Val! your father left you better off than that!"

"But so much of it went, Anne," was the gloomy answer. "I never understood the claims that came in against me, for my part. Edward had no back debts, to speak of; but then look at what his allowance had been."

"He was the eldest son," she gently said.

"I know that. I am not wishing myself in Edward's place, or he out of it. I heartily wish him health and a long life to wear his honours; it is no fault of his that he should be rolling in riches, and I a martyr to poverty. Still, one can't help feeling at odd moments, when the shoe's pinching awfully, that the system is not altogether a just one."

"Was that a sincere wish, Val Elster?"

Val wheeled round on Lady Maude, from whom the question came. She had stolen up to them unperceived, and stood there in her radiant beauty, her magnificent dark eyes and her glowing cheeks surmounted by a little coquettish black-velvet hat.

"A sincere wish—that my brother should live long to enjoy his honours!" echoed Val in a surprised tone. " Indeed it is. I hope he will live to a green old age, and leave goodly sons to succeed him."

Lady Maude laughed. A brighter hue stole into her cheeks, a softer shade to her eyes: she saw herself, as in a vision, the goodly mother of those goodly sons.

"Are you going to wear *that?*" she asked, touching—nay, striking—the knot of ribbon in Miss Ashton's hands with her petulant fingers. "They are Lord Hartledon's colours."

"I shall wear it on Monday. Lord Hartledon gave me the knot."

A rash avowal. The competitors, in a sort of joke, had each given away one knot of his own colours. Lady Maude had had three given to her; but she was looking for another worth them all— from Lord Hartledon. And now—it was given, it appeared, and to Anne Ashton! For her very life she could not have helped the passionate taunt that escaped from her, not in words, but in tone:

"To *you!*"

"Kissing goes by favour," broke from the delicate lips of Val Elster, and Lady Maude could have struck him for the significant, saucy expression of his violet-blue eyes. "Edward loves Anne better than he ever loved his sisters; and for any other love—*that's* far enough off his heart yet, Maude."

She had recovered herself instantly; called out "Yes" to those in the distance, as if she heard a call, and went away humming a tune.

"Val, she loves your brother," whispered Anne.

"Do you think so? I do sometimes; and again I'm puzzled. She acts well if she does. The other day, I told Edward she was in love with him: he laughed at me, and said I was dreaming; that if she had any love for him, it was cousin's love. What's more, Anne, he'd prefer not to receive any other; so Maude need not look after him; it will be labour lost. Here comes that restless Dowager Kirton down upon us! I shall leave you to her, Anne. I never dare say my soul's my own in the presence of that woman."

Val strolled away as he spoke. He was not at

ease that day, and the sharp, meddling old woman would have been intolerable. It was all very well to put a good face on matters to Anne, but he was in more perplexity than he cared to tell of. It seemed to him that he would rather die than give up Anne: and yet—in the straightforward, practical good sense of Dr. Ashton, he had a formidable adversary to deal with.

He suddenly found an arm inserted within his own, and saw his brother. Walking together thus, there was a great resemblance between the brothers. They were of the same height, much of the same make; both were very good-looking men, but Percival had the nicest features; and he was fair, and his brother dark.

"What is this, Val, about a dispute with the doctor?" began Lord Hartledon.

"It was not a dispute," returned Val. "There were a few words, and I was hasty. However, I begged his pardon, and we parted good friends."

"Under a flag of truce, eh?"

"Something of that."

"Something of that!" repeated the earl.

"Don't you think, Val, it would be to your advantage if you trusted me more thoroughly than you do? Tell me the whole truth of your position, and let me see what can be done for you."

"There's not much to tell," returned Val, in his stupidity. Even with his brother his ultra-sensitiveness clung to him; and he could no more have confessed to the extent of his troubles, than he could have taken wing that moment and soared away in the air. Val Elster was one of those who trust to things "coming right" with time.

"I have been talking to the doctor, Val. I called in just now to see Mrs. Ashton, and he spoke to me about you."

"Very kind of him, I'm sure!" retorted Val. "It is just this, Edward. He is vexed at what he calls my idle ways, my waste of time: as if I, a gentleman, but one remove from a nobleman, need plod on, like a city clerk, six days in the week, and no holidays! I know I must do something before I can take Anne; and I will do it: but the doctor need not begin to cry out about cancelling the engagement."

"How much do you owe, Val?"

"I can't tell."

Lord Hartledon thought this an evasion. But it was true. Val Elster knew he owed a great deal more than he could pay; but how much it might be on the whole, he had but a very faint idea.

"Well, Val, I have told the doctor I shall look into matters, and I hope to do it efficiently, for Anne's sake. I suppose the best thing will be to try and get you an appointment again."

"O Edward, if you would! And you know you have the ear of the ministry."

"I daresay it can be managed. But this will be of little use if you are still to remain an embarrassed man. I hear you were afraid of arrest in London."

"Who told you that?"

"Dawkes."

"Dawkes! Then, Edward——" Val Elster stopped. In his vexation, he was about to retaliate on Captain Dawkes by a little revelation on the score of *his* affairs, certain things that might not have redounded to that gallant officer's credit.

But he arrested the words in time: he was of a kindly nature, not fond of returning ill for ill. With all his follies, Val Elster could not remember to have committed an evil act in all his life, save one. And that one he had still the pleasure of paying for pretty deeply.

"Dawkes knows nothing of my affairs except from hearsay, Edward. I was intimate once with the man; but he served me a shabby trick, and that was the ending of the friendship. I don't like him."

"I daresay what he said was not true," said the earl kindly. "You might as well make a confidant of me. However, I have not time to talk to-day; we will go into the thing, Val, after Monday, when this race has come off, and see what arrangement can be made for you. There's only one thing bothers me."

"What's that?"

"The danger that it may be a superfluous arrangement. If you are only set up on your legs to come down again, as you have before, it will be so much waste of time and money;

so much waste, to me, of temper. Don't you see, Val?"

Percival Elster stopped short in his walk, and withdrew his arm from his brother's; his face was working with emotion, his voice trembled with it.

"Edward, I have learnt a lesson. What it has cost me I hardly know yet: but it is *learnt*. On my sacred word of honour, in the solemn presence of Heaven, I assert it, that I will never put my hand to another bill, whatever may be the temptation. I have overcome, in this respect at least, my sin."

"Your sin?"

"My nature's great sin; the besetting sin that has clung to me through life; the unfortunate sin that is my bane to this hour — cowardly irresolution."

"All right, Val; I can see you mean well now. We'll talk of these matters next week. Instead of Elster's Folly, let it be Elster's Wisdom."

Lord Hartledon wrung his brother's hand and

turned away. His eyes fell on Miss Ashton, and he went straight up to her. Putting the young lady's arm within his own, without word or ceremony, he took her off with him to a distance: and bedecked old Lady Kirton's skirts went round in a dance of passion as she saw it.

"I am about to take him in hand, Anne, and set him going again. I have as good as promised it to Dr. Ashton. We must get him a snug berth; one that even the doctor won't object to, and set him straight in other matters. My belief is that he has mortgaged his patrimony; it shall be redeemed. And, Anne, I think——I do think——he may be trusted to keep straight for the future."

Her sweet soft eyes sparkled with pleasure, and her lips parted with a sunny smile. Lord Hartledon took her hand within his own as it lay on his arm, and the furious old Dowager saw it from the distance.

"Don't say so much as this to him, Anne: I only tell you. Val is of so sanguine a nature, that it may be better not to tell him all beforehand. And I want of course, first of all, to get at a true list of—that is, at a true statement of facts;" he broke off, not caring to speak the word debts to that delicate girl before him. "He is my only brother; my father left him to me, for he knew what Val was; and I'll do my best. I'd do it for Val's own sake, apart from the charge. And, Anne, once Val is on his legs with something of an income, snug and comfortable, you know, I shall recommend him to get married without delay; for, after all, you will be his greatest safeguard."

A crimson blush suffused her face, and Lord Hartledon smiled. Down came the Countess Dowager.

"Here's that restless Dowager Kirton calling to me. She never lets me alone. Val sent me into a fit of laughter yesterday, saying she had designs on me for Maude. Poor deluded woman!—Yes, ma'am, I hear. What is it?"

Mr. Elster went strolling along on the banks of the river, towards Calne; not with any particular purpose, but in his restless uneasiness. He had a tender conscience, and his past follies were pressing on it heavily. He felt sure of one thing — that he was more deeply involved than Lord Hartledon or any body else suspected, perhaps himself. The route this way was charming in fine warm weather, though less pleasant in winter. It was by no means a frequented road, rather a solitary one, and belonged of right to Lord Hartledon only; but it was open to all. Few chose it, when they could traverse the straighter way by the road. The narrow path on the green plain, sheltered as it was by trees, wound in and out, now on the banks of the river, now hidden amidst a portion of the wood. Altogether it was a lonely and wild road; not one that a timid nature would choose by preference on a dark night. You might sit in the wood, which lay to the left, a whole day through, and never see a soul.

One little part of the walk was especially beautiful. A green dell, whose turf was soft as moss; open to the river on the right, with a glimpse of the lovely scenery beyond; and on the left, the clustering trees of the dark wood. Beyond, through a vista in the arching trees, which nearly closed it in, might be seen a view of the houses of Calne. A little stream, or rivulet, trickled from the wood, and a rustic bridge —more for ornament than use, for a man with long legs could stride the stream well — was thrown over it. Val had got thus far, when he saw a gentleman standing on the bridge, his arms leaning on the parapet, and apparently in a brown study.

A wild-looking, dark man, whose face, at the first glimpse, seemed all hair. There was certainly a profusion of it; eyebrows, beard, whiskers, all thick, and as black as night. He was attired in loose fustian clothes, with a red handkerchief rather thickly wound round his throat, and a low slouching hat—one of those called a wide-awake—which partially concealed his features. By his side stood another man in plain dark clothes, which, except that they were rather seedy and the coat outrageously long, were of good make and material. He wore a cloth hat, whose brim hid his face, and was smoking a cigar. Both of the men were slightly built and under the middle height, though the loose fustian suit of the other made him look stout rather than thin. This one had red whiskers.

The moment Mr. Elster set eyes on the rough one, he felt conscious he saw the man Pike before him. It happened that he had not met him during these few days of his sojourn; but some of the gentlemen staying at Hartledon had, and had said what a loose sort of man he appeared to be. The other was a stranger, and did not look like a countryman at all.

Mr. Elster saw them both take a sharp look at him as he approached; and then they spoke together. Both stepped off the bridge, as if in deference, for him to pass; but in truth it was hardly wide enough for two abreast on it. They stood aside, watching him come over, and Pike touched his wide-awake.

"Good day, my lord."

Val nodded by way of answer, and continued

his stroll onwards. In the look he had taken at Pike, it struck him he had seen the face before: something in the countenance seemed familiar to his memory. And to his surprise he saw the man was young.

The supposed reminiscence did not trouble him: he was too much occupied with thoughts of his own affairs to have any superfluous leisure for Mr. Pike's. A short way, and this rude, sheltered part of the road terminated in more open ground, where three paths converged: one back to the front of Hartledon; one across to some cottages, and on through the wood to the high road; and one straight along towards the rectory and Calne. Rural paths still, all of them; and the last had a bench or two by its side. Val Elster strolled on nearly to the rectory, and then turned back: he had no errand at Calne, and the rectory he would rather keep out of just now. When he came to the little bridge, Pike was on it alone; the other one had disappeared. As before, he stepped off it to make way for Mr. Elster.

"I beg pardon, sir, for having addressed you just now as Lord Hartledon."

The salutation took Val by surprise; and though the voice was a mumbling sort of voice, as if the man mouthed his words purposely, the accent and language were superior to any thing he might have expected from one of Mr. Pike's appearance and reputed lawless character.

"No offence," said Val, courteous even to Pike, in his kindly nature. "You mistook me for my brother. Many do."

"Not I," returned the man, assuming a freedom, a roughness, at variance with his evident intelligence and his words. "I know you for the Honourable Mr. Elster."

"Ah," said Mr. Elster, a slight curiosity stirring in his mind, but not sufficient to induce him to follow it up.

"But I like to do a good turn if I can," pursued Pike; "and I think, sir, I did one to you in calling you Lord Hartledon."

Val Elster had been passing on. He turned back and looked at the man.

"Are you in any little bit of a temporary difficulty, might I ask?" continued Pike. "No offence, sir; princes have been in such before now."

Val Elster was so supremely conscious, especially in that reflective hour, of being in a "little bit" of difficulty that might prove more than temporary, that he could only stare at the questioner and wait for more.

"No offence again, if I'm wrong," resumed Pike; "but if that man you saw here on the bridge is not looking after the Honourable Mr. Elster, I'm a fool."

"Why do you think this?" inquired Val, too fully aware that the fact was a likely one, to attempt any reproof or disavowal.

"I'll tell you," said Pike; "I've said I don't mind doing a good turn when I can. The man arrived here this morning by the slow six train from London. He went into the Stag and got his breakfast, and has been dodging about in a covert sort of manner ever since. He inquired his way to Hartledon; the landlord of the Stag asked him what he wanted there, and got for answer that his brother was in my lord's service, one of the grooms. Bosh! He went up, sneaking under the hedges and along by-ways, and took a view of the house, standing a good hour behind a tree while he did it. I was watching him."

It instantly struck Percival Elster, by one of those flashes of conviction that are no less sure than subtle, that Mr. Pike's interest in this watching, arose from a fear that the stranger might have been looking after *him*. Pike continued:

"After he had taken his fill of waiting, he came dodging down this way, and I got into conversation with him. He wanted to know who I was. A poor devil out of work, I told him; a soldier once, but maimed and good for little now. We got chatty; I let him think he might trust me, and he began asking no end of questions about the Honourable Mr. Elster: whether he went out much, what were his hours for going out, which road he mostly took in his walks, and by what marks he could know him from his brother the earl; he knew they were alike. The hound was puzzled; he had seen a dozen swells come out of Hartledon, any one of which might be Mr. Elster; but I found he had the description pretty accurate. While we were talking, who should come in view but yourself! 'This is him!' cried he. 'Not a bit of it,' said I carelessly; 'that's my lord.' Now you know, sir, why I saluted you as Lord Hartledon."

"Where is he now?" asked Percival Elster, feeling that he owed his present state of liberty to this lawless man.

Pike pointed to the narrow path in the wood, that led across to the high road. "I filled him up with the belief that the way beyond this bridge up to Hartledon was private, and he might be taken up for trespassing if he attempted to follow it; so he went off that way to watch the front. If the fellow has not got a writ in his pocket, or something worse, call me a born natural. You are all right, sir, as long as he takes you for Lord Hartledon."

But there was little chance that the fellow could long go on taking him for Lord Hartledon, and the Honourable Mr. Elster felt himself attacked with the cold shivers. He knew it was worse than a writ; it was an arrest. An arrest is not a pleasant affair for any one; but a strong opinion—a prevision rather; a certainty—seized hold of Val's mind that this would bring forth Dr. Ashton's veto of separation from Anne.

"I thank you for what you have done," frankly spoke Mr. Elster.

"It's nothing. He'll be dodging about after his prey; but I'll dodge about too, and I'll thwart his game if I can, though I have to swear that Lord Hartledon's not Lord Hartledon. What's an oath, more or less, to me?"

"Where have I seen you before?" asked Val.

"Hard to say," returned Pike. "I have knocked about in many parts in my time."

"Are you from this neighbourhood?"

"No. Never was in these parts at all till a year or so ago. It's not two years yet."

"What are you doing here?"

"What I can. Getting a bit of work when I can get it given to me. I went tramping the country after I left the regiment—"

"Then you have been a soldier!" interrupted Mr. Elster.

"Safe enough. In tramping the country I came upon this place: I crept into a shed, and was there for some days; rheumatism had hold of me, and I couldn't move. It was something to find I had a roof of any sort over my head, and be let lie in it unmolested: and when I got better I stopped on."

"And have adopted it for your own, and have put a window and a chimney in it! But do you know that Lord Hartledon may not choose to retain you for a tenant?"

"If Lord Hartledon should think of ousting me, I'd ask the Honourable Mr. Elster to intercede, in requital for the good turn I've done him this day," was the bold answer.

Mr. Elster laughed. "What is your name?"

"Tom Pike."

"I hear a great deal said of you, Pike, that's not pleasant; that you are a poacher, and a—"

"Let them that say so prove it," interrupted Pike, his black brows contracting.

"But how do you manage to live?"

"That's my business, and not Calne's. At any rate, Mr. Elster, I don't steal."

"I heard a worse hint dropped of you than any I have mentioned," continued Val after a pause.

"Tell it out, sir. Let's have all the catalogue at once."

"That the night my brother, Mr. Elster, was shot, you were out with the poachers."

"I daresay you heard that I shot him, for I know that it has been said," fiercely roared the man. "It's a black, bitter lie!—and the time may come when I shall ram it down Calne's throat. I swear that I never fired a shot that night; I swear that I had no more a hand in George Elster's death than you had. Will you believe me?"

The accents of truth are rarely mistakable, and Val was positive he heard them now. So far, he believed the man; and from that moment dismissed the doubt from his mind, if indeed it had not been dismissed before.

" Do you know who did fire the shot ? "

" I do not ; I was not out at all that night. Calne pitched upon me, because there was nobody else in particular that it could pitch upon. A dozen poachers were in the fray, most of 'em with guns ; little wonder that the random shot from one should have found a mark. I know nothing more certain than that, so help —"

" That will do," interrupted Mr. Elster, stopping what might be coming ; for, as is sometimes the case with men of a refined nature, he preferred simple language to strong. " I believe you fully, Pike. What part of the country were you born in ? "

" London. Born and bred in it."

" That I do not believe," he said frankly. " Your accent is not that of a Londoner."

" As you will, sir," returned Pike. " My mother was of country birth—Devonshire ; but I was born and bred in London. I recognised that one with the writ for a fellow cockney at once ; and for what he was, too,—a sheriff's officer.

Shouldn't be surprised but I knew him for one years ago."

Val Elster dropped a coin into the man's hand, and bade him good morning. Pike spat upon it, touched his wide-awake in token of thanks, and reiterated his intention of "dodging the enemy." But, as Mr. Elster pursued his way with cautious steps, and eyes that peered ten ways at once, the face he had just quitted continued to haunt him. It was not like any face he had ever seen, that he could remember; but nevertheless ever and anon some reminiscence seemed to start out of it and vibrate against a chord in his memory.

CHAPTER VII.

CLERK GUM'S SHUTTERS.

It was a rather singular coincidence, noted after the terrible event, now looming in the horizon, had taken place, and when people began to comment on the various circumstances surrounding it, that Monday, the second day fixed for the boat-race, should be another day of rain. As if heaven would have interposed to prevent it! said the thoughtful and romantic.

A steady, pouring, soaking rain; putting a stop again to the race for that day. The competitors might have been willing to get wet backs, but not to subject the fair spectators to the same. There was some inward discontent, and a great deal of outward grumbling; it did no good, and the race was put off until the next day.

Val Elster retained his liberty as yet. Very chary indeed had he been of showing himself outside the door on Saturday, once he got safely inside it; neither had any misfortune befallen Lord Hartledon. That unconscious peer must have contrived, in all innocence, to "dodge" the gentleman who was looking out for him, for they did not meet.

On the Sunday it happened that neither of the brothers went to church. Lord Hartledon, on awaking in the morning, found himself with a sore throat, and would not get up. Val did not dare to show himself out of doors. Not from fear of arrest that day, but lest any officious meddler should be pointing him out as the real Simon Pure, the Honourable Percival Elster. But for these circumstances, the man with the writ could hardly have remained under the delusion, as he appeared at church himself.

"Which is Lord Hartledon?" he whispered to his neighbour on the free benches, when the large party from the great house had entered, and been settled in their pews.

"I don't see him. He has not come to-day."

"Which is the Honourable Mr. Elster?"

"He has not come, either. He isn't here." So for that day recognition was escaped.

It was not to be so on the next. The rain, as I have said, came pouring down, putting off the boat-race, and keeping Hartledon's guests indoors all the morning; but late in the afternoon some ill-conditioned star put it into the earl's head to go down to the rectory. His throat was better— nearly well; and he was not a man to coddle himself unnecessarily.

He paid his visit, stayed talking a considerable time with Mrs. Ashton, in whose company he liked to be, and took his departure about six o'clock. "You and Anne might almost walk up with me," he remarked to the doctor as he shook hands; for the rector and Miss Ashton were engaged to dine at Hartledon that day. It was to have been the crowning festival to the boat-race— the race which now had not taken place.

Lord Hartledon looked up at the skies, and found he had no occasion to open his umbrella, for the rain had ceased. Sundry rays in the west, increasing in brightness, momentarily seemed to give good hope that the morrow would be fair; and his lordship, rejoicing in this cheering prospect, crossed the broad lawn of the rectory. As he went through the gate, somebody laid a hand upon his shoulder.

" The Honourable Percival Elster, I believe?"

The earl looked at the intruder. A seedy man with a long coat and large red whiskers, who held out something to him.

" Who are you ?" he asked, releasing his shoulder by a dexterous movement.

" I'm sorry to do it, sir; but you know we are but the agent of others in these affairs. You are my prisoner, sir."

" Indeed!" said the earl, taking the matter coolly. " You have got hold of the wrong man for once. I am not the Honourable Percival Elster."

The capturer laughed: a very civil laugh. " It won't do, sir ; we often have that trick tried on us."

" But I tell you I am *not* Mr. Elster," reiterated the peer, speaking this time with some asperity. " I am Lord Hartledon."

He of the loose coat shook his head. He

had his hand again on the supposed Mr. Elster's arm, and told him he must go with him.

" You cannot take me; I am a peer of the realm. This is simply ridiculous," continued Lord Hartledon, almost laughing at the real absurdity of the thing. " Any child in Calne could tell you who I am."

" As well make no words over it, sir. It's only waste of time."

" You have a warrant—as I understand—to arrest the Honourable Percival Elster?"

" Yes, Mr. Elster, I have. The man that was looking for you in London got taken ill, and couldn't come down here, and our folks sent me. ' You'll know him by his good looks,' said they; ' an aristocrat, every inch of him.' Don't give me trouble, sir."

" Well now—I am not Percival Elster: I am his brother, Lord Hartledon. You cannot take one brother for another; and, what's more, you had better not try. Stay! look here."

He pulled out his card-case, and showed his cards—" The Earl of Hartledon." He exhibited a couple of letters that happened to be about him —" The Right Honourable the Earl of Hartledon." It was of no use.

"I've known that dodge tried before, too," said his obstinate capturer.

Lord Hartledon was getting angry. He saw some convincing proof must be tendered before he could have his liberty. Jabez Gum happened to be standing at his gate opposite, and the earl called to him.

"Will you be so kind as tell this man who I am, Mr. Gum. He is mistaking me for some one else."

"This is the Earl of Hartledon," said Jabez promptly.

A moment's hesitation on the officer's part; but he felt too sure of his man to believe this. "I'll take the risk," said he stolidly. "Where's the good of your holding out, Mr. Elster?"

"Come this way, then!" cried the earl, beginning to lose his temper. "And if you carry this too far, my man, I'll have you punished."

He went striding up to the rectory. Had he

taken a moment for consideration, he might have turned away instead, rather than expose this misfortune of Val's there. The doctor came into the hall, and was recognised as the rector, and there was some little commotion; Anne's white face looking on at it from a distance. The man was convinced, and took his departure in humility, considerably crest-fallen.

"What is the amount?" called out the doctor sternly.

"Not over-much, sir, *this*. It's under three hundred."

Which was as much as to say that there was more behind it. Dr. Ashton mentally washed his hands of the Honourable Percival Elster as a future son-in-law.

The first intimation that ill-starred honourable gentleman received of the untoward turn affairs were taking, was from the rector himself. Mr. Percival Elster had been chuckling over that opportune sore throat, as a blessed means of keeping his brother indoors; and it never occurred to him that Lord Hartledon would venture out at all on the Monday. Being a man with his wits about him, it, of course, had not failed to occur to his mind that there was a possibility of Lord Hartledon's being arrested in place of himself; but so long as the earl kept indoors, the danger was averted. Had Percival Elster seen his brother go out, he might have plucked up the courage to tell him the state of affairs.

But he did not see him. Lounging idly—what else had he, a poor prisoner, to do?—in the sunny society of Maude Kirton, and of other attractive girls, Mr. Elster was unconscious of the movements of the household in general. He was in his own room dressing for dinner when the truth burst upon him.

Dr. Ashton was a straightforward, practical man—it has been already said so—who went direct to the point at once in any matters of difficulty. He arrived at Hartledon a few minutes before the dinner-hour, found Mr. Elster was yet in his dressing-room, and went there to him.

The news, the cool scornful anger of the rector, the keen question—"Was he mad?" burst upon the unhappy Val like a clap of thunder. He was standing in his shirt-sleeves, so white and nice; ready to go down, all but his coat and waistcoat, and his hair-brush in the one uplifted hand. The hand and the brush had been arrested midway in the shock. The calm clerical man; all the more terrible then because of his calmness; standing there with his cold stinging words, and the unhappy *taken-to* culprit facing him, conscious of his heinous sins—the worst sin of all, that of being found out.

"Others have done as much before me, sir, and have not made the less good men," spoke Val in his desperation.

Dr. Ashton could not help admiring the man, as he stood there in his physical beauty. In spite of his inward anger, his condemnation, his disappointment—and they were all very great— the good looks of Percival Elster struck him forcibly with a sort of annoyance: why should these men be so fair outwardly, so frail inwardly? Those good looks had told upon his daughter's heart; and they all loved *her*, and could not bear to cause her pain. Tall, supple, graceful, and strong, towering nearly a head above the doctor, he stood, his pleasing features full of the best sort of attraction, his violet eyes rather wider open than usual, the waves of his silken hair smooth and bright. "If he were only half as fair in conduct as in looks!" muttered the grieved divine.

But those violet eyes, usually beaming with kindness to all the world, suddenly changed their present expression of deprecating softness for one of angry rage. Dr. Ashton gave a pretty accurate description of how the crisis had been brought to his knowledge—that Lord Hartledon had come to the rectory, with his mistaken assailant, to be identified; and Percival Elster's anger was turned against his brother. Never in all his life had he been in such a passion; and the having to suppress its signs in the presence of the rector only made the fuel burn more fiercely. To ruin him with the doctor by going *there* with the news! Any where else!—any where else!

Hedges, the butler, interrupted the conference. Dinner was waiting. Lord Hartledon looked to

Val as the two entered the room, and was rather surprised at the furious gaze of reproach that was cast back on him.

Miss Ashton was not there. No, of course not! It needed not Val's glance round to be assured of that. Of course they were to be separated from that hour; the fiat was already gone forth. And Mr. Val Elster felt so savage that he could have struck his brother. He heard Dr. Ashton's reply to an inquiry—that Mrs. Ashton was feeling unusually poorly, and Anne remained at home with her—but he looked upon it as an evasive excuse. Not a word did he speak during dinner: not a word, save what was forced from him by the commonest courtesy, spoke he after the ladies had quitted the room; he only drank a great deal of wine.

A very unusual circumstance for Val Elster. With all his weak resolution, his yielding nature, unseemly drinking was a fault he was scarcely ever seduced into. Not above two or three times in his life could he remember to have exceeded the bounds of strict, temperate sobriety. The fact was, he was in wrath with himself: all his past follies were pressing upon him with condemnatory bitterness. He was just in that frame of mind when an object to vent our fury upon becomes a kind of necessity; and Mr. Elster's was vented on his brother.

He was waiting at boiling-point for the opportunity to "have it out" with him: and it soon came. As the gentlemen left the dining-room— and in these present days they do not, as a rule, sit long, especially when the host is a young man —Perceival Elster touched his brother to detain him, and slammed the door on the heels of the rest.

Lord Hartledon was surprised. Val's attack was so savage. He was talking off his superfluous wrath, and the wine he had taken did not tend to cool his heat. Lord Hartledon, vexed at the injustice, lost his temper; and for once there was a quarrel, sharp and loud, between the brothers. It did not last long: in its very midst they parted; throwing cutting words the one at the other. Lord Hartledon quitted the room, with a sneer, to join his guests; Val Elster strode outside the window to cool his brain.

But now, look at the obstinate pride of those two foolish men! They were angry with each other in temper, but not in heart. In Percival Elster's conscience there was an underlying conviction that his brother had acted only in thoughtless impulse when he carried the misfortune to the rectory; while Lord Hartledon was even then full of plans to serve Val, and considered he had more need to help him than ever. A day or two given to the indulgence of their tempers, and they would be firmer friends than before.

The large French window of the dining-room, opening to the ground, was flung back by Val Elster; and he stepped forth into the cool night, which was beautifully fine. The room looked towards the river. The velvet lawn, wet with the day's rain, lay calm and silent under the bright stars; the flowering exotics, clustering around far and wide, gave out their sweet and heavy night perfume. Not an instant had he been outside when he became conscious that some figure was gliding towards him—was almost close; and he recognised Mr. Pike. Yes, that worthy gentleman appeared to be only then arriving on his evening visit: in point of fact, he had been glued ear and eye to the window during the quarrel.

"What do you want?" demanded Mr. Elster.

"Well, I came up here hoping to get speech of you," replied the man in his rough, abrupt manner, more in character with his appearance and his lawless reputation than with his natural accent and unmistakable intelligence. "There was a nasty accident came off a few hours ago: that shark caught hold of his lordship."

"I know he did," savagely spoke Val. "The result of your information to him that I was Lord Hartledon."

"I did it for the best, Mr. Elster. He'd have nabbed you that very time, but for my putting him off the scent as I did."

"Yes, yes, I am aware you did it for the best, and I suppose it turned out to be so," quickly replied Val in an impulse of justice, some of his native kindliness resuming its sway. "It's an unfortunate affair altogether, and that's the best that can be said of it."

"What I came up here for was to tell you he was gone."

"Who is gone?"

"The shark."

"Gone!"

"He went off by the seven train. Lord Hartledon told him he'd communicate with his principals and see that the affair was arranged. It satisfied the man, and he went away by the next train—which happened to be the seven-o'clock one."

"How do you know this?" asked Mr. Elster.

"This way," was the answer. "I was hovering about outside that shed of mine, and I saw the encounter at the parson's gate—for that's where it took place. The first thing the fellow did when it was all over was to come bolt over the road to me, and accuse me of purposely misleading him. 'Not a bit of it,' said I; 'if I did mislead you, it was unintentional, for I took the one who came over the bridge on Saturday to be Lord Hartledon, safe as eggs. But they have been down here only a week,' I went on, ' and I suppose I don't know 'em apart yet.' I can't say whether he believed me; I think he did: he's a soft sort of chap. It was all right, he said: the earl had passed his word to him that it should be made so without his arresting Mr. Elster, and he was off back to London at once."

"And he has gone?"

Mr. Pike gave a significant nod of the wide-awake on his bushy black head. "I watched him go. I dodged him up to the station and saw him off."

Then this one danger was over! He, Val, might breathe freely again.

"And I thought you would like to know that the coast was clear, so I came up to tell it," concluded Pike.

"Thank you for your trouble," said Mr. Elster. "I shall not forget it."

"You'll remember it perhaps, if a question arises touching that shed," spoke the man. "I may need a word sometime with Lord Hartledon."

"I'll remember it, Pike. Here, wait a moment. Is Thomas Pike your real name?"

"Well, I conclude it is. Pike was the name of my father and mother. As to Thomas—not knowing where I was christened, I can't go and look at the register; but they never called me any thing but Tom. Did you wish to know particularly?"

There was a tone of mockery in the man's answer, not particularly acceptable to his hearer; and he let him go without further word. But the man turned back in an instant of his own accord.

"I daresay you are wanting to know why I did you this little turn, Mr. Elster. I have been caught in corners myself before now; and if I can help any body to get out of 'em without trouble to myself, I'm willing to do it. And to circumvent these law-sharks comes home to my spirit as a wholesome refreshment."

Mr. Pike finally departed. He took the lonely way, and only struck into the high road opposite his own domicile, the shed. Passing round it, he hovered at its rude door—the one he had himself made, along with the more rude window—and then treading softly and gingerly, he stepped to the low stile in the hedge, which had for years made the boundary between the waste-land on which the shed stood and Clerk Gum's garden. Here he halted a minute, looking all ways. Then he stepped over the stile, crouched down amid Mr. Gum's cabbages, until he was like a cabbage himself, got under shelter of the back hedge, and so stole onwards, until he came to an anchor at the kitchen-window, and laid his ear to the protecting shutter, just as it had recently been laid against the glass in the dining-room of my Lord Hartledon.

That he had a propensity for prying into the private affairs of his neighbours near and distant, there could be little doubt. Mr. Pike, however, was not destined on this one occasion to reap any substantial reward. The kitchen appeared to be wrapped in perfect silence. Satisfying himself as to this, he next took off his heavy shoes, stole past the back-door, and so round the clerk's house to the front. Very, very softly indeed went he, creeping by the wall, and emerging at last round the angle, by the window of the best parlour. Here, very excessively to Mr. Pike's consternation, he came upon a lady doing exactly what he had come to do — namely, stealthily listening at the window to any thing there might be to hear inside.

The shrill scream she gave when she lifted her face and found it in contact with the wild black-haired one of the other intruder, might have been heard over at Dr. Ashton's. Clerk Gum, who had been quietly writing in his office, came out in haste, and recognised Mrs. Jones, the wife of the surly porter at the station, and the step-mother of the troublesome young servant, Becca. Pike had totally disappeared.

Mrs. Jones, partly through her startled state of fright, partly in passion, arising from a long-standing grievance, avowed the truth boldly: that she had been listening at the parlour-shutter ever since she went out of the house ten minutes ago, and had been set upon by that wolf, Pike.

"Set upon!" exclaimed the clerk, looking swiftly in all directions for the offender.

"I don't know what else you can call it, when a highway robber—a murderer, if all tales is true—steals round upon you without warning, and glares his eyes into yours," shrieked Mrs. Jones wrathfully. "And if he wasn't barefoot, Gum, my eyes strangely deceived me. I'd have you and Nancy take care of your throats."

She turned into the house, to the best parlour, where the clerk's wife was sitting with a visitor, Mary Mirrable. Mrs. Gum, when she found what the commotion had been about, cried out with a sharp cry of terror, and shook from head to foot.

"On our premises! Close to our house! That dreadful man! O Lydda, don't you think you mistook?"

"Mistook! Me!" retorted Lydda Jones, whose tongue could be tolerably free on occasion. "That wild black face ain't one to be mistook: I should like to see its fellow in Calne. Why Lord Hartledon don't have him took up on suspicion of that murder, is odd to me."

"You'd better hold your tongue about that

suspicion, Lydda," interposed Mary Mirrable. "I have cautioned you before. I'd not like to breathe a word against a desperate man; I should go in fear that he might hear of it, and avenge himself."

In came the clerk. "I don't see a sign of any body about," he said; "and I'm sure whoever it was could not have had the time to get away. You must have been mistaken, Lydda Jones."

"Me mistaken! Mistaken in what, pray?"

"That any man was there. You got confused, and fancied it, perhaps. As to Pike, he'd never dare to come on my premises, whether by night or by day. What were you doing at the window?"

"Listening," defiantly replied Mrs. Lydda—a corruption of Lydia. "And now I'll just tell out what I've had in my head this long while, Jabez Gum, and know the reason of Nancy's slighting me in the way she do. What secret have she and Mary Mirrable got between them?"

"Secret?" repeated the clerk, while his wife

gave a faint cry, and Mary Mirrable turned her calm face on Mrs. Jones. " Have they a secret ?"

" Yes they have," raved Mrs. Jones, giving vent to her long pent-up passion and temper. " If they haven't, I'm blind and deaf. If I have come into your house once during the past year and found Mary Mirrable stuck in it, and the two sitting and whispering, I've come ten times, Jabez Gum. This evening I came in at dusk; I turned the handle of the door and peeped into the best parlour, and there they were, nose and knees together, starting away from each other as soon as they saw me, and Nance giving one of her faint cries, and the two making believe to have been talking of the weather. It's always so. And I want to know what secret it is that they have got hold of, and whether I'm poison, that I can't be trusted with it."

Jabez Gum slowly turned his eyes on the two in question. His wife lifted her hands in deprecation at the thought that she should have a secret: Mrs. Mirrable (as she was called in Calne) was laughing.

"Nancy's secret to-night, when you interrupted us, was telling me of a dream she had, regarding Lord Hartledon, and of how she mistook Mr. Elster for him the morning he came down," cried the latter. "And if you have really been listening at the shutters since you went out, Lydda, you should by this time know how to pickle walnuts in the new way: for I declare that is all our conversation has been about since. You always were suspicious, you know, and you always will be."

"Look here, Mrs. Jones," said the clerk decisively; "I don't choose to have my shutters listened at: it might give the house an ill name, for quarrelling, or something of that. So I'll trouble you not to repeat what you have done to-night, or I shall forbid your coming here. A secret, indeed!"

"Yes, a secret!" persisted Mrs. Jones, in her aggravating obstinacy. "And if I don't come at what it is one of these days, my name's not Lydda. It strikes me — I may be wrong — but it strikes me it concerns me and my husband and my household, which some folks are ever ready to interfere with. I'll take myself off now; and I'd recommend you, as a parting warning, to denounce that Pike to the police for an attempt at housebreaking, afore you be both battered senseless in your bed. It'll be the end on't."

She went away, screaming out the last words down the garden-path. Clerk Gum wished he could denounce *her*. Mary Mirrable laughed again; and the other woman, so cowardly timid, fell back in her chair as one taken in an ague-fit.

Beyond giving an occasional dole to Mrs. Jones for her children—and to tell the truth, she clothed the lot, or they would have gone naked—Mary Mirrable had shaken her cousin off long ago: which of course did not tend to soothe the naturally cranky and jealous spirit of Mrs. Jones. Hartledon House she was not welcomed at, and could not go to it; but she looked out for the visits of Mary Mirrable at the clerk's, and was certain to intrude herself in there also on those occasions.

"I'll find it out!" she repeated to herself, as

she went banging through the garden-gate; "I'll find it out. And as to that there hairy poacher of a Pike, he'd better bring his black face a-nigh mine again!"

CHAPTER VIII.

THE WAGER BOATS.

TUESDAY morning rose, bright and propitious: a contrast to the two previous days fixed on for the boat-race. All was pleasure, bustle, excitement at Hartledon: but the coolness that had arisen between the brothers was noticed by some of the guests. Neither of them was disposed to be conciliatory, or to take the first step towards reconciliation: and, indeed, a little incident that occurred that morning led to another ill word between them. An account that had been standing for more than two years was sent in to Lord Hartledon's steward; it was for some harness, a saddle, a silver-mounted whip, and a few trifles of that sort, supplied by a small tradesman in the village. Lord Hartledon protested there was nothing of the kind owing; but upon inquiry the debtor proved to be the Honourable Percival Elster. Lord Hartledon, vexed that any one in the neighbourhood should have been made to wait so long for his money, said a sharp word on the score to Percival; and the latter retorted as sharply that it was no business of his. Again Val was angry with himself, and thus gave vent to his temper. The fact was, he had completely forgotten the trifling debt, and was as vexed as Lord Hartledon that it should have been allowed to remain unpaid: but the man had not sent him any reminder while he was away.

"Pay it to-day, Marris," cried Lord Hartledon to his steward. "I'll not have this sort of thing at Calne."

The tone of his voice was one of aggravation—or at least it sounded so in the ears of his conscious brother, and Val bit his lips. After that, throughout the morning, they maintained a studied silence to each other; and this was observed, but was not commented on. Val was unusually quiet altogether: he was saying to himself that he was sullen.

The starting hour for the race was three o'clock; but long before that, the scene was sufficiently animated, not to say exciting. It was a most lovely afternoon. Not a trace remained of the previous day's inopportune rain; and the river—wide just there, as it took the sweeping round of the point—was dotted with these little wager boats. Their lordly owners for the time being, in their white boating costume, each displaying his colours, were in the highest spirits; and the fair gazers gathered on the banks were anxiously eager as to the result. The favourite was Lord Hartledon—by long odds, as Mr. Shute grumbled. Had his lordship been known not to possess the smallest chance, nine of those fair girls out of ten would, nevertheless, have betted upon him. Some of them were hoping to play for a deeper stake than the winning of a pair of gloves—that of being mistress of Hartledon. A staff, from which fluttered a gay little burgee, had been driven into the ground, exactly opposite the house: it was the starting and the winning point. At a certain distance up the river, near to the mill, a boat was moored in midstream: this they would row round, and come back again.

At three o'clock they were to take the boats; and, allowing for time being wasted in the start, might be in again and the race won in three-quarters of an hour. But, as is often the case, the time was not adhered to; one hindrance occurred after another; there was a great deal of laughing and joking, and forgetting of things and of getting into order; and at a quarter to four they were not off.

But all was ready at last, and most of the rowers were, each in his little cockle-shell of a boat. Lord Hartledon lingered yet. He was in the midst of the group of ladies, all clustered together at one spot; they were keeping him with their many comments and questions. Each one wore the colours of her favourite: crimson and purple predominating, for they were those of the earl. Lady Kirton displayed her loyalty in a conspicuous manner: she had an old crimson gauze skirt on, a ball-dress once, with ends of purple ribbon floating out from it and fluttering in the wind, as you may have seen a strong breeze sometimes take a horse's tail; and a purple head-dress with a crimson feather. Maude, in a spirit of perversity, displayed a blue shoulder-knot, timidly offered to her by a young Oxford man who was staying there, Mr. Shute; and Anne Ashton wore the colours given her by Lord Hartledon.

"I can't stay; you'd keep me all day: don't you see they are waiting for me?" he laughingly cried, extricating himself from the throng. "Why, Anne, my dear, is it you? How is it I did not see you before? Are you here alone?"

She had not long joined the crowd, having come up late from the rectory, and had been standing outside, for she never pushed herself forward any where. Lord Hartledon drew her arm within his own for a moment and took her apart.

"Arthur came up with me: I don't know where he is now. Mamma was afraid to venture; she thought the grass might be damp."

"And the rector *of course* would not countenance us by coming," said Lord Hartledon with a laugh. "I remember his prejudices against boating of old."

"He is coming to dinner."

"As you all are; Arthur also to-day. I made the doctor promise that. A jolly banquet we'll have, too, and toast the winner. Anne, I just wanted to say this much: Val is in an awful rage with me for letting that matter get to the ears of your father, and I am not pleased with him; so altogether we are just now treating each other to a dose of sullenness, and when we do speak it's to growl, like two amiable bears; but it shall make no difference to what I said last week. All shall be rendered smooth, even to the satisfaction of your father. You may trust to me."

He ran from her, stepped into the skiff, and was taking the sculls, when he uttered a sudden exclamation, leaped out again, and began to run with all speed towards the house.

"What is it? Where are you going?" asked

that tall fine man the O'Moore, so thoroughly Irish, and who was the appointed steward.

" I have forgotten — " *What*, they did not catch; the word was lost on the air.

" It is bad luck to turn back," called out Maude. " You won't win."

He did not hear; he was already half-way to the house. A couple of minutes after entering it, he reappeared again, and came flying down the slopes at the speed of a racehorse. All in a moment his foot slipped, and he fell to the ground. The only one who saw the accident was Mr. O'Moore; the general attention at that moment being concentrated upon the river. He hastened back. His lordship was then gathering himself up, but slowly.

" No damage," said he; " only a bit of a wrench to the foot. Give me your arm for a minute, O'Moore. This ground must be slippery from the rain yesterday."

Mr. O'Moore held out his arm, and the Earl took it. " The ground is not slippery, Hart; it's as dry as a bone."

"Then what caused me to slip?"

"The speed you were coming at. Had you not better give up the contest, and rest?"

"Nonsense! My foot will be all right in the skiff. Let me get along; they'll be out of patience."

When it was seen that something was amiss with him, that he leaned, and rather heavily, on the O'Moore, anxious questions were directed to him, eager steps pressed round him. Lord Hartledon laughed, making light of it: he had been so clumsy as to stumble, and it had twisted his ankle a little. 'T was nothing.

"Stay on shore and give it a rest," cried one of them, as he stepped once more into the little boat. "I am sure you are hurt."

"Not I. It will have rest in the boat.—Anne," he said, looking up to her with his pleasant smile, "do you wear my colours still?"

She touched slightly the handsome knot on her bosom, and smiled back to him, her tone one of earnestness. "I would wear them always."

And the Countess Dowager, in her bedecked

spreading flounces and her crimson feather, looked as if she would like to throw the knot into the river, in the wake of the wager boats. Which got off at last, after one or two false starts.

"Do you think it is seemly, this flirtation of yours with Lord Hartledon?"

Anne turned in amazement. The face of the old Dowager was close at her ear; the snub nose and the rouged cheeks and the false flaxen front looked ready to eat her.

"I have no flirtation with Lord Hartledon, Lady Kirton; or he with me. When I was a child, and he a great boy, years older, he loved me and petted me as a little sister: I think he does the same still."

"My daughter tells me you are counting upon one of the two—the earl or his brother. If I say to you, do not be too sanguine of either, I speak as a friend; as your mother might speak. Lord Hartledon is already appropriated; and Val Elster is not worth appropriating."

Was she mad? Anne Ashton looked at her, really doubting it. No, she was only vulgar-minded, and selfish, and utterly impervious to all sense of shame in her scheming. Instinctively Anne moved a pace further off.

" I do not think Lord Hartledon is appropriated yet," spoke Anne, in a little spirit of mischievous retaliation. " That some amidst his present guests would be glad to appropriate him may be likely enough; but what if he is not willing to be appropriated? He said to Mr. Elster last week, that they were wasting their time."

" Who's Mr. Elster?" cried the angry Dowager. " What right has he to be at Hartledon, poking his nose into every thing that does not concern him?—what right has he, I ask?"

" The right of being Lord Hartledon's brother," carelessly replied Anne.

" It is a right he had best not presume upon," scornfully rejoined Lady Kirton. " Brothers are brothers as children; it can't be helped when they are in the same common home, and it's right it should be so; but the tie becomes wide and loose as they grow up and launch out abroad into their different spheres. There's not a man of all

Hartledon's guests but has more right to be here than Val Elster. It is not good for him, the contrast: the one a peer of the realm, rich and powerful; the other a poor obscure fellow, that must get his bread and cheese before he eats it."

"Yet they are brothers still."

"Brothers! I'll take care that Val Elster presumes no more upon the tie, when Maude reigns at Hartledon. I'll —"

For once the Countess Dowager caught up the words on her tongue. She had said more than she had meant to say. Anne Ashton's calm sweet eyes were bent upon her, waiting for more.

"It is true," she said, giving a shake to the purple tails, and taking a sudden resolution, "Lady Maude is to be his wife; but I ought not to have let it slip out. It was unintentional; and I throw myself on your honour, Miss Ashton."

"But it is not true?" asked Anne, somewhat perplexed.

"It *is* true. Hartledon has his own reasons for keeping it quiet at present; but—you'll see when the time comes. Should I take upon myself so much rule here as I am doing, but that it is to be Lady Maude's future home?"

"I don't believe it," cried Anne stoutly, as the old story-teller sailed off. "That she loves him, and that her mother is anxious for him, is all true; but he is truthful and open, and would never conceal it. No, no, Lady Maude! you are nourishing a false hope. You are very beautiful, but you are not worthy of him; and I should not like you for my sister-in-law at all. That dreadful old Countess Dowager! how she dislikes Val, and how rude she is! I'll try and not come in her way again after to-day, as long as they are at Hartledon."

"What are you thinking of, Anne?"

"O, not much," she answered, with a soft blush, for the questioner was Mr. Elster. "Do you think your brother has hurt himself much, Val?"

"I didn't know he had hurt himself at all," returned Val rather coolly, who had been on the river at the time in somebody's skiff, and saw nothing of the occurrence. "What has he done?"

"He slipped down on the slopes and twisted his ankle. I suppose they will be coming back soon."

"I suppose they will," was the answer. Val seemed in an ungracious mood. He and Mr. O'Moore and young Carteret were the only three who had remained. Anne asked Val why he did not go and look on at the race; and he answered, because he didn't want to.

It was getting on for five o'clock when the boats were discerned returning. How they clustered on the banks, watching the excited rowers, some pale with their exertions, others in a white heat! Captain Dawkes was first, and was doing all he could to keep so; but when only a boat's-length off the winning-post, another shot past him and won by half a length. It was the young Oxonian, Mr. Shute—though indeed it does not much matter who it was, save that it was not Lord Hartledon.

"Strike your colours, ladies, you that sport

the crimson and purple!" called out a laughing voice from one of the skiffs. "Oxford blue wins."

His lordship arrived last. He did not get up for some minutes after the rest were in. In short, he was distanced.

"Hart has hurt his arm as well as his foot," observed one of the others, as he came alongside. "That's why he got distanced."

"No, it was not," dissented his lordship, looking up from his skiff at the crowd of fair faces bent down upon him. "My arm is all right; it only gave me a few twinges when I first started. My oar fouled, and I could not get right again; so, finding I had lost too much ground, I gave up the contest.—Anne, had I known I should disgrace my colours, I would not have given them to *you*."

"Miss Ashton loses, and Lady Maude wins!" cried out the Countess Dowager, executing a little dance of triumph, which made her look not unlike a huge peacock turning itself about in the rays of the declining sun. "Maude is the only one who displays the Oxford blue."

It was true. The young Oxonian was a retiring and timid man, and none had voluntarily assumed his colours. But nobody was paying heed to the Countess Dowager.

"You are like a child, Hartledon, denying that your arm's damaged!" exclaimed Captain Dawkes. "I know it is: I could see it by the way you struck your oar all along."

What feeling is it in man that prompts him to disclaim physical pain?—to make light of personal damage? Lord Hartledon's ankle was swelling to the size of two, at the bottom of the boat; and there's not the slightest doubt his arm *was* paining him, though perhaps at the moment not very considerably. But he maintained his own assertion. He protested his arm was as sound as the best arm present. "I could go over the work again with pleasure," cried he.

"Nonsense, Hart! You could not."

"And I *will* go over it," he added, warming with the opposition. "Who'll try his strength with me? There's plenty of time before dinner."

"I will," eagerly spoke young Carteret, who

had been, as was remarked, one of the stayers on shore, and was wild to be handling the oars. "If Dawkes will let me have his skiff, I'll bet you ten to one you are distanced again, Hart."

Perhaps Lord Hartledon had not thought his challenge would be taken seriously. But when he saw the eager, joyous look of the boy Carteret—he was not yet nineteen—the flushed pleasure of the beardless face, he would not have retracted it for the world. He was just as good-natured as Percival Elster.

"Dawkes will let you have his skiff, Carteret."

Captain Dawkes was exceedingly glad to be rid of it. Good boatman though he was, he rarely cared to spend his strength superfluously, when nothing was to be gained, and had no fancy to row his skiff to the place where it was kept, as most of the others were already doing by theirs. He leaped out.

"Any body but you, Hartledon, would be glad to come out of that tilting thing, and enjoy a rest, and get your face cool," cried the Countess Dowager.

"I daresay they might, ma'am. I'm afraid I am given to obstinacy; always was. Be quick, Carteret."

Mr. Carteret was hastily stripping himself of his coat, and any odds and ends of attire he deemed he could do without. "One moment, Hartledon; only one moment," came the joyous response.

"And you'll come home with your arm and your ankle the hue of your colours, Hartledon — crimson and purple," screamed the Dowager. "And you'll be laid up, and go on perhaps to lockjaw; and then you'll expect me to nurse you!"

"I shall expect nothing of the sort, ma'am, I pledge you my word; I'll nurse myself. — All ready, Carteret?"

"All ready. Same point as before, Hart?"

"Same point: round the boat and home again."

"And it's ten sovs. to one, you know, Hart?"

"All right; ten sovs. to one. You'll lose your one, Carteret."

Mr. Carteret laughed. He saw the ten sovereigns as surely in his possession as he saw the two sculls in his hand. There was no trouble with the start this time, and they were off at once.

Lord Hartledon taking the lead. He was spurring his exertions to the uttermost: perhaps out of bravado; that he might show them nothing was the matter with his arm. But Mr. Carteret gained on him; and as they turned the point and got out of sight, the young man's boat was the foremost.

The race had been kept—as the sporting men amidst them styled it—dark. Not an inkling of it had been suffered to get abroad, or, as Lord Hartledon had observed, they should have the banks swarming. The consequence was, that not more than half-a-dozen curious idlers had gathered: those were on the opposite side, and had now gone down with the ruck of boats to Calne. No spectators, either on the river or the shore, attended on this smaller contest: Lord Hartledon and Mr. Carteret had it all to themselves.

And meanwhile, during the time Lord Hartledon had remained at rest in his skiff under the winning flag, Percival Elster never addressed to him one word. There he stood, on the edge of the bank; but not a syllable spoke he, good or bad.

Miss Ashton was looking out for her brother. She might just as well have looked for a needle in a bottle of hay. Arthur was off somewhere.

"You need not go home yet, Anne," said Val.

"I must. I have to dress for dinner. It is all to be very grand to-night, you know," she said, with a merry laugh.

"With Shute in the post of honour. Who'd have thought that awkward, quiet fellow would win? I will see you home, Anne, if you must go."

Miss Ashton coloured vividly with embarrassment. In the present state of affairs, she did not know whether that might be: poor Val was in ill odour at the rectory. He detected the feeling, and it tended to vex him more and more.

"Nonsense, Anne! The veto has not yet

been interposed, and they can't kill you for allowing my escort. Stay here if you like: if you go, I shall see you home."

It was quite imperative that she should go, for the dinner at Hartledon was that evening fixed for seven o'clock, and there would be little enough time to dress and come back again. They set off, walking side by side. Anne told him of what Lord Hartledon had said to her that day; and Val coloured with shame at the sullenness he had displayed, and his heart went into a glow of repentance. Had he met his brother then, he had clasped his hand in warmth, and poured forth his contrition.

He met some one else instead, almost immediately. It was Dr. Ashton, who was coming for Anne. Percival was not wanted now: was not invited to continue his escort. A cold, civil word or two passed, and Val struck across the grove into the high road, and returned that way to Hartledon. Perhaps he thought he had had enough of the soft grass for that day, and would try the hard road by way of a change.

He was about to turn in at the lodge-gates and give his usual joking greeting to Mrs. Capper — that industrious lady being at her open window in a state of soap-suds up to the elbows — when his attention was caught by a figure coming down the avenue. A man in a long coat that flapped about his heels, and his cheeks ornamented with bushy red whiskers. It required no second glance for a recognition: the whiskers and the coat proclaimed their owner at once; and if ever the Honourable Val Elster's heart leaped into his mouth, it certainly took the leap then.

He went on, instead of turning in; went quietly, as if he were but a stranger enjoying an evening stroll up the road; but the moment he was quite past the gates, he set off at a break-neck speed, not heeding where. That the man was looking after him to arrest him, he felt as sure as he had ever felt of any thing in this world; and in his perplexity he began accusing every body of treachey, Lord Hartledon and Pike in particular.

The river at the back in this part took a sweeping curve, bowing round on the road, as it were; the road went straight; so that to arrive at a given point, the one would be a great deal more quickly traversed than the other. On and on went Val Elster; and as soon as an opening allowed, he struck into the brushwood on the right, intending to make his way back by the river to Hartledon.

But not yet awhile. Not until the shades of night should be falling on the earth: he would have a better chance of getting away from that shark by dark than by daylight. He propped his back against a tree and waited, hating himself all the while for his cowardice. With all his scrapes and dilemmas, he had never been reduced to hiding, such as this.

And his pursuer had struck into the wood after him, passed straight through it, though with some little doubt and difficulty, and was already by the river-side, getting there just as Lord Hartledon was passing in his skiff. Long as this may have seemed in telling, it was but a short time in the action; still Lord Hartledon had not made quick way, or he would have been further on his course in the race.

Would the sun ever set?—daylight ever pass? Val thought *not,* in his impatience; and he ventured out of his shelter very soon, and saw for his reward—the long coat and the red whiskers on the river's brink, their owner in converse with a man. Val tore off further away, keeping the direction of the stream: the brushwood might no longer be safe. He did not think they had seen him: the man he dreaded had his back to him, the other had his face. And that other one was Pike.

CHAPTER IX.

WAITING FOR DINNER.

THE dinner at Hartledon had been ordered for seven o'clock. It was beyond that hour when Dr. Ashton arrived, for he had been detained—a clergyman's time is not always under his own control. Anne and Arthur were with him, but not Mrs. Ashton. He came in, ready with an apology for his tardiness, but found he need not offer it; neither Lord Hartledon nor his brother having yet appeared.

"Hartledon and that boy Carteret have not returned home yet," said the Countess Dowager, in her fiercest tones, for she was fonder of her dinner than of any earthly thing, and could not brook the being kept waiting for it. "And when they do come, they'll keep us another half-hour while they dress."

"I beg your ladyship's pardon — they are come," interposed Captain Dawkes. "Carteret was going into his room as I came out of mine."

"Time they were," grumbled the Dowager. "They were not, five minutes ago, for I sent to ask Hartledon's man."

"Which of the two won the race?" inquired Lady Maude of Captain Dawkes.

"I don't think Carteret did," he replied, laughing. "He seemed as sulky as a bear, and growled out that there had been no race, for Hart had served him a trick."

"What did he mean?"

"Goodness knows."

"I hope Hartledon upset him," charitably interrupted the Dowager. "A ducking would do that boy Carteret good; he is too forward by half."

There was more waiting. The Countess Dowager flounced about in her florid gown of pink satin; but it did not bring the loiterers any the sooner. Lady Maude — perverse still, but very beautiful — talked in a whisper to the hero of the day, Mr. Shute; and she wore a blue-silk robe and a blue wreath in her hair. Anne adhered to the colours of Lord Hartledon, though he had been defeated; she was in a rich and glistening white silk, natural flowers of red and purple on its body and sleeves, and the same in her hair. Her sweet face was sunny again; her eyes were sparkling: a word dropped by Dr. Ashton had given her a hope that, perhaps, Percival Elster might be forgiven sometime.

He was the first of the culprits to make his appearance. The Dowager, who was getting ravenous, attacked him of course. What did he mean by keeping the dinner waiting?

Val replied that he was late in coming home; he had been out. As to keeping the dinner waiting, it seemed that Lord Hartledon was doing that: he didn't suppose they'd have waited for him.

He spoke tartly, as if not on good terms with himself or the world. Anne Ashton, near to whom he had drawn, looked up at him with a charming smile.

"Things may brighten, Percival," she softly breathed.

"It's to be hoped they will," gloomily returned Val. "They look dark enough just now."

"What have you done to your face?" she whispered.

"To my face? Nothing that I know of."

"The forehead is red, as if it had been bruised, or slightly grazed."

Val put his hand up to his forehead. "I did feel it smart when I washed it just now," he remarked slowly, as though doubting whether any thing was amiss or not. "It must have been done—when I—struck against that tree," he added, apparently rummaging his recollection.

"How was that?"

"I was running fast in the dusk, and did not notice the branch of a tree in my way. It's nothing, Anne; the redness will soon go off."

Mr. Carteret came in, looking just as Val Elster had done—out of sorts. Questions were showered upon him as to the fate of the race; but the Dowager's voice was heard above all.

"This is a pretty time to make your appearance, sir! Where's Lord Hartledon?"

"He's in his room, I expect. Hartledon never came," he added, his tone a very sulky one, as he turned from her to the rest. "I rowed on, and on, thinking how nicely I was distancing him, and got down, the mischief knows where. Miles, nearly, I must have gone."

"But why did you go beyond the boat—the turning-point?" asked one.

"There was no boat," returned Mr. Carteret; "some confounded meddler must have unmoored it as soon as the first race was over, and I, like an idiot, rowed on, looking for it. All at once it came into my mind what a way I must have gone, and I turned and waited. And might have waited till now," added Mr. Carteret, in an access of temper," for Hart never came."

"Then his arm must have failed him," exclaimed Captain Dawkes. "I thought it was all wrong."

"It wasn't right, for I soon shot beyond him, out and out," returned young Carteret, more and more aggrieved at every word. "But Hart knew the spot where the boat ought to have been, though I didn't; what he did, I suppose, was to clear round it just as though it had been there, and come in home again. It will be an awful shame if he takes an unfair advantage of it, and claims the race."

"Hart never took an unfair advantage in his life," spoke up Val Elster, in a clear, decisive tone. "You need not be afraid, Carteret. I daresay his arm failed him."

"Well, he might have hallooed out to me when he found it failing, and not have suffered me to row all that way for nothing," was the retort of young Carteret. "Not a trace could I see of him as I came back; he had hastened home, I expect, to shut himself up in his room with his damaged arm and foot."

"I'll see what he's doing there," said Val.

He went out; but returned immediately. The little snub nose of the Dowager turned up with a sniff of hope.

"We are all under a mistake," was the greeting of Val. "Hartledon has not returned yet. His servant is in his room waiting for him."

"Then what do you mean by telling stories?" demanded the Countess Dowager, turning sharply on Mr. Carteret in her angry hunger.

"Good heavens, ma'am! you need not begin upon me!" was the retort of young Carteret. "I have told no stories. I said Hart let me go on, and never came on himself; if that's a story, I'll swallow Dawkes's skiff and both the sculls."

"You said he was in his room. You know you did."

"I said I expected so. It is usual for a man to go there, I believe, to make himself decent for dinner," added young Carteret, always ripe for a wordy war, in his antipathy to the Countess Dowager.

"*You* said he had come in;" and the angry woman faced round on Captain Dawkes. "You saw them going into their rooms, you said. Which was it—that you did, or you didn't?"

"I did see Carteret; and I certainly assumed that Lord Hartledon had gone into his," replied the captain, suppressing a laugh. "I am sorry to have misled your ladyship. I daresay Hart is about the house somewhere."

"Then why doesn't he show himself?" stormed the Dowager. "Pretty behaviour this, to keep a score of people waiting for dinner. I shall tell him so.—Val Elster, open the door, and call Hedges."

Val rang the bell. "Has Lord Hartledon come in?" he asked, when the butler appeared.

"No, sir."

"And the dinner's spoiling, isn't it, Hedges?" broke in the Dowager.

"It won't be any the better for waiting, my lady."

"No. I must exercise my privilege as the house's mistress, and order it served. At once, Hedges, do you hear? If Hartledon grumbles, I shall tell him it serves him right."

"But where can Hartledon be?" cried Captain Dawkes.

"That's what I am thinking of," said Val. "He can't be on the river all this time; Carteret would have seen him in coming home."

A strangely grave shade, looking almost like a prevision of evil, arose to Dr. Ashton's face. "I trust nothing can have happened to him," he exclaimed. "Where did you part company with him, Mr. Carteret?"

"That's more than I can tell, sir. You must have seen—at least—no, you were not here; but those who were looking must have seen me get ahead of him within view of the starting-point; soon after that I lost sight of him. The river winds, you know; and of course I thought he was coming on behind me. A great daft I must have been, not to divine that the boat had been removed!"

"Do you think he passed the mill?"

"The mill?"

"That place where the river forms, one may almost say an arm, a miniature harbour. A mill is built there which the stream serves. You could not well fail to see it."

"I remember now. Yes, I saw the mill. What of it?"

"Did Lord Hartledon pass it?"

"Law bless you, I don't know!" cried the boy; "I had lost sight of him ages before that."

"The current is extremely rapid there," observed Dr. Ashton. "If he found his arm fail him, he might strike down to the mill and land; and his ankle may be keeping him a prisoner there."

"And that's what it is!" exclaimed Val.

They were crossing the hall to the dining-room. Without the slightest ceremony, the Countess Dowager pushed herself foremost and advanced to the head of the table.

"I shall occupy this seat in my nephew's absence," said she. "Dr. Ashton, will you be so good as take the foot? There's nobody else to do it."

"Nay, madam; though Lord Hartledon may not be here, Mr. Elster is."

She had actually forgotten Val; and she would have liked to ignore him now that he was recalled to her remembrance; but that might not be. As much of contempt as could be expressed in her face was expressed in it, as she turned her snub nose and her small round eyes in defiant silence upon that unoffending younger brother.

"I was going to request you to take it, sir," said Perceival in a low tone to Dr. Ashton. "I shall go off in the pony-carriage for Edward. He must think we are neglecting him."

"Very well. I hate those rowing matches," heartily added the rector.

"What a curious old fish that parson must be!" ejaculated young Carteret to his next neighbour. "He says he doesn't like boating."

It happened to be Arthur Ashton, and the lad's brow lowered. "You are speaking of my father," he said. "But I'll tell you why he does not like it. He had a brother once, a good deal older than himself; they had no father, and Arthur—that was the eldest's name—was very fond of him: there were only those two. He took him out in a boat one day, and there was an accident: the eldest was drowned, the little one saved. Do you wonder that he—papa—has dreaded boating ever since? He seems to have the same sort of dread of it that a child who has been frightened by its nurse has of the dark."

"By Jove! that was a go, though!" was the sympathising comment of Mr. Carteret.

The doctor was saying grace, and the dinner proceeded. It was not half over when Mr. Elster came in, in his light over-coat. He walked straight up to the table, and stood by it, his face wearing a blank, perplexed look. A momentary silence of expectation, and then many tongues were loosed together.

"Where's your brother? Where's Lord Hartledon? Has he not come?"

"I don't know where he is," answered Val. "I was in hopes he had reached home before me, but I find he has not. I can't make it out at all."

"Did he land at the mill?" asked Dr. Ashton.

"Yes, he must have done that, for the skiff is moored there."

"Then he's all right," interrupted the doctor; and there was a strangely-marked sound of relief in his tone: as that of one who has escaped from some great pain to a great joy.

"O, he is all right," confidently asserted Percival. "The only question is, where he can be. The miller was abroad this afternoon, and left his place locked up; so that Hartledon could not get in, and had nothing for it but to start home with his lameness, or sit down on the banks until somebody found him."

"He must have set off to walk."

"I should think so. But where has he walked to?" added Val. "I drove slowly home, looking on either side of the road, but could see nothing of him."

"What should bring him on the side of the road?" demanded the Dowager, speaking with her mouth full. "Do you think he would make himself into a tramp, and take his seat on a mound of stones? Where do you get your ideas from, Val Elster?"

"From common-sense, ma'am. If he set off to walk, and his foot failed him midway, he'd have nothing for it but to sit down and wait. But he is *not* on the road: that is the curious part of the business."

"Would he come the other way?"

"Hardly. It is so much further by the river than by the road."

"You may depend upon it that is what he has done," said Dr. Ashton. "He might think he should meet some of you that way, and get an arm to help him."

"I declare I never thought of that," exclaimed Val, his face brightening. "There he is, no doubt; perched somewhere between this and the mill, like patience on a monument, unable to put foot to the ground."

He turned away. Some of the gentlemen offered to accompany him; but he declined their help, and begged them to go on with their dinners, saying he would take sufficient servants with him, even though they had to carry Lord Hartledon.

So Mr. Elster went, taking servants and lanterns; for in some parts of this road the trees overhung it, and rendered it dark. But they could not find Lord Hartledon. They searched, and shouted, and showed their lanterns: all in vain. Very much perplexed indeed, did Val Elster look when he got back again.

"Where in the world can he have gone to?" angrily questioned the Countess Dowager, who by no means approved of these repeated interruptions to her beloved meal; and she glared from her seat at the head of the table on the offender Val, as she asked it. "I must say all this is most unseemly, and Hartledon ought to be brought to his senses for causing it. I suppose he has taken himself off to a surgeon's."

It was possible, but unlikely, as none knew better than Mr. Elster. To get to the surgeon's he would have to pass his own house, and would be more likely to go in, and send for Mr. Hillary, than walk on, with a disabled foot. Besides, if he had gone to the surgeon's, he would not be staying there all this while. "I don't know what to do," said Percival Elster; and there was the same blank, perplexed look on his face that was observed the first time he came in. I do not much like the appearance of things."

"Why, you don't think there's any thing

wrong with him!" exclaimed young Carteret, starting from his chair with an alarmed face. "He's safe to turn up, isn't he?"

"O, of course he will turn up," answered Val, in a dreamy tone. "Only this uncertainty, as to where to look for him, is not pleasant."

Dr. Ashton motioned Val to his side. "Are you fearing an accident?" he asked, in a low tone.

"No, sir."

"*I am.* That current by the mill is so fearfully strong; and if your brother had not the use of his one arm—and the boat was drawn onwards, beyond his control—and upset—"

Dr. Ashton paused. Val Elster looked rather surprised.

"How could it upset, sir? The skiffs are as safe as this floor. I don't fear that in the least: what I do fear is that Edward may be in some out-of-the-way nook, insensible from the pain, and won't be found until daylight. Fancy, a whole night out of doors, and alone, in that state! He might be half dead of cold by morning."

Dr. Ashton shook his head in dissent of this

view. His dislike of boating seemed just now to be rising into horror.

"What are you going to do now, Elster?" inquired Captain Dawkes.

"Go to the mill again, I think, and find out if any body saw Hartledon leave the skiff, and which way he took. One of the servants can run down to Mr. Hillary's the while."

"But you'll snatch a mouthful of dinner first," cried the Countess Dowager, ungraciously.

"I have no time, ma'am. He may be waiting somewhere for his."

Dr. Ashton rose, bowing for permission to Lady Kirton; and the gentlemen with one accord rose with him, the same purpose in the mind of all —that of more effectually scouring the ground between the mill and Hartledon. The Countess Dowager, who had by no means finished her dinner, felt that she should have liked to box the ears of the lot. The idea of real fear, in connection with Lord Hartledon, had not yet penetrated her brain.

At this moment, before they had left the room,

there arose a strange wild sound from without—half howl, half wail — an unearthly noise, that seemed to come from several voices, and to be bearing round the house from the river-path. Mrs. O'Moore threw down her knife and fork, and rose up with a shriek.

"There's nothing to be alarmed at," said the Dowager to her. "It is those Irish harvest-labourers. I know their horrid voices, and I daresay they are riotously drunk. Hartledon ought to put them in prison for it."

The sounds died away into silence. Mrs. O'Moore took her hands from her eyes, where they had been pressed. "Don't you know what it is, Lady Kirton? It is the Irish death-howl!"

It rose again, louder than before, for those from whom it came were nearing the house—a frightful, howling, wailing noise, ringing out awfully clear in the silence of the night. Mrs. O'Moore cowered down in her chair again, and hid her face of terror. She was not Irish born, and had never heard that sound but once, and that was when her child died.

"She says true," cried her husband, the O'Moore; "that is the death-wail. Hark! it is for a chieftain; they mourn the loss of one high in the land. And — they are coming here! O Elster! can DEATH have overtaken your brother?"

The gentlemen had stood spell-bound, listening to the noise, their faces a mixture of surprise and credulity. At the words, they rushed out with one accord, and the women stole after them with trembling steps and blanched lips.

"If ever I saw such behaviour in all my existence!" irascibly spoke the Countess Dowager, who was left alone in her glory, and deep in a delicious serving of grouse. "The death-wail, indeed! The woman's a fool. I'll get those drunken Irishmen transported, if I can."

In the hall were gathered the servants, cowering almost as the ladies did. Their master had flown down the hall-steps, and the Irish labourers were coming steadily up to it, bearing something in procession. Dr. Ashton came back as quickly as he had gone out, extending his arms before him.

"Ladies, I pray you go in," he urged in strange agitation. "You must not meet these — these Irishmen. Go back to the dining-room, I entreat you, and remain in it."

But the curiosity of women—who can suppress it? They were as though they heard him not, and were pressing on to the door, when Val Elster dashed in with a white face.

"Back, all of you! You must not stay here. This is no place or sight for you. Anne," he added, seizing Miss Ashton's hand in peremptory entreaty, "you at least know how to be calm. Get them away, and keep them out of the hall."

"Tell me the worst," she implored. "I will indeed try to be calm. Who is it those men are bringing here?"

"My dear brother—my dead brother. Madam," he continued, catching hold of the Countess Dowager, who had now come out, her dinner-napkin in her hand, and her curls all awry, "you must not come here. You must all go back to the dining-room."

"Not come out here! Go back into the dining-room!" repeated the outraged Dowager. "Don't take quite so much upon yourself, Val Elster. The house is Lord Hartledon's, not yours, and I presume I am a free agent in it. I suppose Hartledon's coming in with his leg swollen as big as that pillar. I sha'n't faint at the sight."

A shriek—an awful shriek—burst from Lady Maude. In her agony of suspense she had stolen out unperceived, and lifted the covering of the rude bier, now resting on the steps. The rays of the hall-lamp fell on the face that was underneath, and Maude, in her heartfelt anguish, with a succession of low hysterical sobs, came shivering back to sink down at her mother's feet.

"O, my love—my love! Dead! dead!"

The only one who heard the whole of the words was Anne Ashton. The Countess Dowager caught the last.

"Who is dead? What is this mystery?" she asked, unceremoniously lifting her satin dress to the waist, with the intention of going out to see, and her head began to nod—perhaps with apprehension—as if she had the palsy. "You want to force us away. No, thank you; not until I've come to the bottom of this."

"Let us tell them," cried young Carteret, in his boyish impulse, "and then perhaps they will go. An accident has happened to Lord Hartledon, ma'am, and these men have brought him home."

"He—he—*he*'s not dead?" asked the old woman in a changed tone.

"Alas! poor Lord Hartledon was indeed dead. The Irish labourers, in passing near the mill, had detected the body in the water; had rescued it, and brought it home.

The Countess Dowager's grief commenced rather turbulently. She talked and shrieked, and danced round in her pink satin in the middle of the hall, exactly as if she had been a wild Indian. It was so intensely ludicrous, that the hall gazed in silence.

"Here to-day, and gone to-morrow!" she sobbed. "Oh—o—o—o—o—o—oh!"

"Nay," cried young Carteret, "here to-day, and gone *now*. Poor fellow! it is awful."

"And you have done it!" she cried, turning

her grief upon the astonished boy, and beginning to dance round him. "You! What business had you to allure him off again in that miserable boat, once he had got home?"

"Don't trample me down, please," he indignantly returned; "I am as cut up as you can be. —Hedges, hadn't you better get Lady Kirton's maid here? I think she's going mad."

"And now the house is without a master," she bemoaned, returning to her own griefs and troubles, "and I have all the arrangements thrown upon myself."

"The house is not without a master," said young Carteret, who seemed inclined to have the last word. "If one master has gone from it, poor fellow! there's another to replace him; and he is at your elbow now."

He at her elbow was Val Elster. Lady Kirton gathered in the sense of the words, and gave a cry; a real prolonged cry of absolute dismay.

"*He* can't be its master."

"I should say he *is*, ma'am. At any rate he is the Earl of Hartledon."

She looked from one to the other in helpless doubt. It was a contingency that had never so much as once occurred to her. Had she wanted confirmation, the next moment brought it to her from the lips of the butler.

"Hedges," called out Percival sternly, in his embarrassment and grief, "open the dining-room door. We *must* get the hall clear."

"The door is open, my lord."

"Yah—ah—ah!" shrieked the Countess Dowager; "*he* Lord Hartledon! Why, I was going to recommend his brother to ship him off to Canada for life."

It was altogether an unseemly scene at such a time. But nearly every thing that the Countess Dowager of Kirton did was unseemly.

CHAPTER X.

MR. PIKE'S VISIT.

PERCIVAL ELSTER was in truth the Earl of Hartledon. By one of those unexpected calamities, which are often unexplainable—and which most certainly was so as yet in the present instance— the life of a promising young nobleman had been snapped asunder, and another had risen into his place. In one short hour Val Elster, who had scarcely cross or coin to call his own, who had been going in danger of arrest from one minute to another, had become a peer of the realm and a wealthy man.

As they laid the body down in a small convenient room opening from the hall, and the gentlemen, his late companions and guests, crowded around in awe-struck silence, there was one amidst them who could not control his grief and emotion. It was poor Val. Pushing aside the others, never heeding them in his bitter sorrow, he burst into a storm of sobs as he leaned over the corpse. And none of them thought the worse of Val for it.

"O Percival! how did it happen?"

The speaker was Dr. Ashton. He was little less affected himself, and he clasped the young man's hand in token of mourning sympathy.

"I cannot think *how* it could have happened," replied Percival, when he could control his feelings sufficiently to speak. "It seems awfully strange to me—mysteriously so."

"If he found himself going wrong, why didn't he shout out?" asked young Carteret, with a rueful face. "I couldn't have been off hearing him."

It was the question that was passing in the minds of all; that was being whispered on their tongues: How could it have happened? The body presented the usual appearance of death from drowning; but close upon the left temple there was a wound, and the face was otherwise disfigured. It must have been done, they thought, by his coming in contact with something or other in the water; perhaps the skiff itself. Arm and ankle were both much swollen.

Nothing was certainly known as yet of Lord Hartledon from the time Mr. Carteret parted company with him, to the time when the body was found. It appeared that these Irish labourers were going home from their work, singing as they went, their road lying past the mill, when they were spoken to by the miller's boy. He was standing on the sort of estrade which abutted on the river, and which the miller had placed there for his own convenience, bending down as far as his young head and shoulders could reach, and peering into the water attentively. "I think I see some'at in the stream," quoth he, and the men stopped; and after a short while, but not at first, they thought they saw "some'at," and they proceeded to search. It proved to be the dead body of Lord Hartledon, caught amidst the thick reeds.

It was rather a curious coincidence that Percival Elster and his servants in the last search should have heard the voices of these labourers singing in the distance. But they were too far off on their return to Hartledon to be within hearing when the men found the body.

The news spread; people came up from far and near, and Hartledon was besieged. Mr. Hillary, the surgeon, gave it as his opinion that the wound on the temple, no doubt caused before death, had rendered Lord Hartledon insensible, and unable to extricate himself from the water. This mill and cottage were built on what might be called an arm of the river. Lord Hartledon had no business there at all; but the current was very strong; and if, as was too probable, he had become almost disabled, he might have been drifted to it without being able to help himself; or it might have been that he was making for it, intending to land and rest in the cottage until help could come to convey him home. How he got into the water was not known. Once in the water, the blow was easy enough: he might have struck against the estrade.

There is nearly sure to be some miserable coincidence in these cases to render them doubly unfortunate. For three weeks past, as the miller testified—a respectable man, of the name of Floyd—his mill had not been deserted; somebody, man, or boy, or woman, had always been at it: on this afternoon it was closed, mill and cottage too, and all were away. What might have been simply a slight accident, had help been at hand, had terminated in an awful death for the want of it.

It was eleven o'clock at night before any thing like order was restored at Hartledon, and the house left in quiet. The last person to quit it was Dr. Ashton. Hedges, the butler, had been showing him out, and was standing for a minute on the steps looking after him, and perhaps to get a little fresh air on his perplexed brow—for the man was a faithful retainer, and the affair had shocked him in no common degree—when he was accosted by Pike, who emerged stealthily from behind one of the outer pillars, where he seemed to have been sheltering.

"Why, what have you been doing there?" exclaimed the butler.

"Mr. Hedges, I've been waiting there—hiding, if you like to call it so," was the answer; and it should be observed that the man's manner, quite unlike his usual rough, devil-may-care tone, was characterised by singular respect and earnestness. To hear him, and not to see him, you might think you were listening to some friend of the family, staid and respectable. "I have been standing there this hour past, keeping behind the pillar while other folks went in and out, and waiting my time to get speech of you."

"Of me?" repeated Hedges.

"Yes, sir, of you. I want you to grant me a favour; and I hope you'll pardon my boldness in asking it."

Hedges did not know what to make of this. It was the first time he had enjoyed the honour of a personal interview with Mr. Pike; and the contrast between that gentleman's popular reputation and his present tone and manners struck the butler as exceedingly singular. But that the butler was in a very softened mood, feeling full of subdued charity to all the world, he might not have condescended to parley with the man.

"What is the favour?" he inquired.

"I want you to get me in to see the poor young earl—what's left of him."

"To get you in to see the earl!" echoed Hedges in his surprise. "I never heard such a bold request."

"It is bold. I've already said so, and asked you to pardon it."

"What can you want that for? It can be for nothing but curiosity, and—"

"It is not curiosity," interrupted Pike, with an emphasis that told upon his hearer. "I have got a different motive, sir; and a good motive. If I were at liberty to tell it—which I'm not—you'd let me in without another word. Lots of people have been seeing him, I suppose."

"Indeed 'lots' of people have not. Why should they? It is a bold thing for *you* to come and ask it."

"Did he come by his death fairly?" whispered the man.

"Good heavens!" exclaimed the butler, stepping back aghast. "I don't think you know what you are talking of. Who would have harmed Lord Hartledon?"

"Let me see him," implored the man. "It can't hurt him or any body else. Only just for a minute, sir, in your presence. And if it's ever in my power to do you a good turn, Mr. Hedges, I'll do it. It doesn't seem likely now; but the mouse gnawed at the lion's net, you know, until he set him free."

Whether it was the singular impressiveness with which the request was proffered, or that the softened mood of Hedges rendered him incapable of contention, certain it was that he granted it; and most likely would wonder at himself for it all his after-life. Crossing the hall with a softened tread, and catching up a candle as he went, he led the way to the room; Mr. Pike stepping after him with a tread equally soft.

"Take your hat off," peremptorily whispered the butler; for that worthy had entered the room with it on. "Is that the way to——?"

"Hedges!"

Hedges was struck with consternation at the call, for it was that of his new master. He had not bargained for this; he had supposed him to be shut in his room for the night. However he might have been foolishly won over to accede to the man's strange request, it was not to be supposed it would be approved of by Lord Hartledon. The butler hesitated. He did not care to show that Pike was there, neither did he care to leave Pike alone.

"Hedges!" came the call again, louder and quicker.

"Yes, sir—my lord;" and Hedges squeezed out at the door without opening it much—which was rather a difficulty, seeing he was a portly man, with a red, honest sort of face—leaving Pike and the light inside. Lord Hartledon—as we must unfortunately call him now—was standing in the hall.

"Has Dr. Ashton gone?"

"Yes, my lord."

"Did he leave that address?"

Hedges knew to what his master alluded: an address that was wanted in connection with certain official proceedings that must now take place. Hedges replied that Dr. Ashton had not left it with him.

"He must have forgotten it," observed the new peer. "He said he would write it down in pencil. Send over to the rectory for it the first thing in the morning. And, Hedges—"

At this moment a slight noise was heard inside the room, like the sound of an extinguisher falling; as, in fact, it was. Lord Hartledon turned to it.

"Who is there, Hedges?"

"I—it—it's no one in particular, sir—my lord."

What with the butler's bewilderment on the sudden change of masters, and what with his self-consciousness of the presence of his visitor, he was unusually confused. Lord Hartledon noticed it. It instantly occurred to him that one of the ladies, or perhaps one of the women-servants, had got admittance to the room; and he did not consider it a proper sight for either.

"Who is it?" he demanded, somewhat peremptorily.

So Hedges had nothing for it but to confess what had taken place, and that he had allowed the man to enter.

"Pike! Why, what can he want?" exclaimed Lord Hartledon in surprise. And he turned to the room.

The moment the butler left him alone, Mr. Pike's first proceeding had been to cover his head again with his wide-awake hat, which he had evidently removed with reluctance, and might have refused to remove at all had it been consistent with policy; his second, was to snatch up the candle, bend over the dead face, and examine it minutely both with eye and hand.

"There *is* a wound there, then, and it's true what they are saying. I thought it might have been the gossip of lying tongues," he muttered, as he pushed the soft dark hair from the temple. "Any more suspicious marks?" he resumed, taking a rapid cursory view of the hands and head, all of the body that was uncovered; for it would be left as it was found until the coroner's inquest. "No; no more. Nothing but he'd likely get in the water: but—I'll swear *that* might have been the blow of a human hand. 'Twas easy enough. 'Twould stun, if it wouldn't kill; and then, held under the water until—"

At this moment Mr. Pike and his pleasant comments were interrupted, and he drew back from the table on which the body was lying; but not before the Earl of Hartledon had seen him fingering the face of the dead.

"What are you doing?" came the stern demand.

"I wasn't harming him," was the answer; and Mr. Pike seemed to have suddenly returned to his roughness. "It's a nasty accident to have happened; and I don't like *this*."

He pointed to the temple as he spoke. Lord Hartledon's usually good-natured brow—at present a brow of deep sorrow—contracted with displeasure.

"It is an awful accident," he replied. "But I asked what you were doing here?"

"I thought I'd like to look upon him, sir; and the gentleman let me in. I wish I'd been a bit nigher the place at the time: I'd have saved him, or I'd have got drowned myself. Not much fear of that, though. I'm a rat for the water. Was that done fairly?" pointing again to the temple.

"What do you mean?" exclaimed the earl.

"Well—it might be, or it might not. One who has led the roving life that I have, and been in all sorts of scenes, and bred in the slums of London too, looks on the suspicious side of these things. And there mostly is one in 'em all."

Lord Hartledon was moved to anger. "How dare you attempt to raise so infamous a suspicion, Pike? If—"

"No offence, my lord," interrupted Pike— "and it's my lord that you are now. Thoughts may be free in this room; but I am not going to spread the suspicion outside. I say, though that *might* have been an accident, it might have been done by an enemy."

"Did you do it?" retorted the earl in his displeasure.

Pike gave a short laugh.

"I did not. I had no cause to harm him. What I'm thinking was, whether any body else had. He was mistaken for another yesterday," continued Pike, dropping his voice, and turning to face the earl. "Some men in his lordship's place might have showed fight then: even blows."

Percival, Lord Hartledon, made no immediate rejoinder. He was gazing at Pike just as fixedly as the latter gazed on him. Did the man wish to insinuate that the unwelcome visitor—the shark— had again mistaken the one brother for the other, and the result had been a struggle between them, ending in this? The notion rushed into the mind of the earl, and a dark flush overspread his face.

"You have no grounds for thinking that man —you know who I mean—attacked my brother a second time?"

"No, I have no grounds for it," shortly answered Pike.

"He was near the spot at the time; I saw him there," continued Lord Hartledon, speaking apparently to himself; while the flush, painfully red and dark, was increasing rather than diminishing.

"I know you did," returned Pike.

The tone grated on his lordship's ear. It implied that the man might become familiar, if not checked; and, with all Percival's good-natured affability, he was not one to permit it; besides, his position was changed, and he could not help feeling that it was. "Necessity makes us acquainted with strange bed-fellows," says the true proverb; and what might have been borne yesterday would not be to-day. Then he was the persecuted Val Elster, hiding himself ignominiously from sharks, and fain to put up with many things in his helplessness. Now he was the powerful Earl of Hartledon.

"Let me understand you," he said, and there was a haughty decision in his tone and manner that surprised Pike. "Have you any cause whatever to suspect that man of having injured, or attempted to injure my brother?"

"*I*'ve not," answered Pike, with a stress upon the I. "I never saw him nearer to the mill yesterday than he was when you looked at us. I don't think he went nearer. My lord, if I knew aught against the man, I'd tell it out, and be glad. I hate all the tribe. *He* wouldn't make the mistake again," added Pike, half contemptuously. "He knew which was his lordship fast enough to-day, and which wasn't."

"Then what did you mean by insinuating that the blow on the temple was the result of violence?"

"I didn't say it was: I said it might have been. I don't know a thing, as connected with this business, against a mortal soul. It's true, my lord."

"Perhaps, then, you will quit this room," said Lord Hartledon.

"I'm going. And many thanks to your lordship for not having turned me from it before, and for letting me have my say.—Thanks to *you*, sir," he added, as he went out of the room and passed Hedges, who was waiting in the hall.

Hedges closed the door after him, and turned to receive a reprimand from his new master.

"Before you admit such men as that into the most sacred chamber the house at present contains, you will ask my permission, Hedges."

Hedges attempted to excuse himself. "He was so very earnest, my lord; he declared to me he had a good motive in wanting to come in. At these times, when one's heart is almost broke with a sudden blow, one is apt to be soft and yielding. What with that feeling upon me, and what with the fright he put me in——"

"What fright did he put you in?" interrupted Val.

"Well, my lord, he—he asked me whether his lordship had come fairly by his death."

"How dare you repeat any such insinuation?" broke forth Lord Hartledon, with more temper than Hedges had ever seen him display. "The very idea is absurd; it is wicked; it is unpardonable. My brother had not an enemy in the world. Take you care not to repeat it again. Do you hear?"

He turned away from the astonished man, and went into the room he had called sacred, and closed the door. Hedges wondered whether the hitherto sweet-tempered, easy-mannered younger brother had changed his nature with his inheritance.

Few, if any, more particulars were elicited as to the cause of accident, as the days went on. That the unfortunate nobleman had become partly, if not wholly, disabled, so as to be incapable of the management of even the little skiff, had been drifted by the current towards the mill, and there upset, was assumed by all to have been the true history. There appeared no cause to doubt that it was such. The inquest was held on the Thursday. And on that same morning the new Earl of Hartledon received a proof of the kindness of his brother. A letter arrived from Messrs. Kedge and Reck, solicitors, the employers of the "shark." It was addressed to the Earl of Hartledon, meaning Edward Earl of Hartledon. By it Percival found—there was no one else to open it now—that his brother had written to them early on the Tuesday morning, taking the debt upon himself; and they now wrote to say they accepted his responsibility, and had withdrawn the officer from Calne. Alas! Val Elster could have dismissed him himself now.

He sat with bent head and drooping eyelids. None, save himself, knew how bitter were the feelings within him, or the remorse that was his portion for having behaved unkindly to his dead brother within the last few hours of life. He had rebelled at his state of debt becoming known to Dr. Ashton; he had feared to lose Anne: it seemed to him now, that he would live under the doctor's displeasure for ever, that he would never see Anne again, could he recall his brother. O, these unavailing regrets! will they rise up to face us at the Last Day?

With a suppressed ejaculation that was like a cry of pain, as if he would throw from him these reflections and could not, Lord Hartledon drew a sheet of paper before him and penned a note to the lawyers. He briefly stated what had taken place; that his brother was dead from an accident, and he had inherited, and should take speedy measures for the discharge of any liabilities there might be against him: and he requested, as a favour, that the letter written to them by his brother might be preserved and returned to him: he should wish to keep it as the last lines his hand had penned.

CHAPTER XI.

THE INQUEST.

On this day, Thursday, the inquest was held. Most of the gay crowd staying at Hartledon had already taken flight; Mr. Carteret, and one or two more, whose testimony might be wished for, remaining. The coroner and jury assembled in the afternoon, in a large boarded apartment called the steward's room. Lord Hartledon was present with Dr. Ashton and other friends: they were naturally anxious to hear the evidence that could be collected, and gather any light there might be to gather. The doors were not closed to the public, and no end of a crowd pressed in: gentle and simple, tag-rag and bob-tail.

The surgeon spoke to the supposed cause of death—drowning: the miller spoke to his house and mill having been that afternoon shut up. He and his wife went over in their spring-cart to Garchester, and left the place locked up, he said. The coroner asked whether it was his custom to lock up his place when he went out; he replied that it was, when they both went out together; but that event happened very rarely. Upon his return, at dusk, he found the little skiff loose in the stream, and he secured it: it was his servant-boy, David Ripper, who called his attention to it first of all. He saw nothing of Lord Hartledon, and had not very long secured the skiff when the Honourable Mr. Elster—as he was then; his lordship now—came up in the pony-carriage, asking if his brother was there. He looked at the skiff, and said it was the one his lordship had been in. Mr. Elster said he supposed his brother was walking home, and he should drive slowly back and look out for him. Later Mr. Elster returned: he had several servants with him then and lanterns; they had come out to look for Lord Hartledon—not the road way, the other way—but could not find him. It was only just after they had gone away again that the Irish harvest-men came up and found the body.

This was the substance of the miller's evidence; it was all he knew: and the next witness called was the boy, David Ripper, popularly styled in the neighbourhood young Rip, in contradistinction to his father, a day-labourer. He was an urchin of ten or twelve, with a red, round face; quite ludicrous from its present expression of terrified consternation. The coroner sharply inquired what he was frightened at; and the boy burst into a roar of sobs, by way of answer. He didn't know nothing, and he hadn't see'd nothing, and it wasn't him that drownded his lordship; and he couldn't tell more, not if they hunged him for 't.

The miller interposed. The boy was one of the idlest young vagabonds he had ever had the luck to be troubled with; and he thought it exceedingly likely he had been off that afternoon and not near the mill at all. He had ordered him to take two sacks into Calne; but when he got home he found the sacks untouched, lying outside where he had placed them. Mr. Ripper had, no doubt, been playing the rover on his own account.

At this accusation Mr. Ripper only howled the louder. The coroner threatened him with a flogging, and the beadle shook him: not with very much effect. The boy was really and truly suffering from terror.

"I can't make him out," exclaimed the miller, regarding his servitor with wondering eyes. "Of all the audacious, hardened lads I ever had to do with, he's the worst in a general way; nothing daunts him. What's took him now?"

"Where did you pass Tuesday afternoon during your master's absence?" sternly demanded the coroner. "Take your hands from your face and answer me, David Ripper."

David Ripper obeyed in the best manner he was capable of, considering his agitation. "I dun know where I was," he said; "I was about."

"About where?"

Mr. Ripper apparently could not say where. He thought he was "setting his bird-trap" in the stubble-field; and he see a partridge, and watched where it scudded to; but he warn't a-nigh the mill the whole time.

"Did you see any thing of Lord Hartledon when he was in the skiff?"

But that the idea was absurd, it might have been thought Mr. Ripper was cognisant of the skiff's doings—had drowned Lord Hartledon, for the matter of that—so utterly did the question destroy his self-possession. His eyes grew large and round, his red face became crimson, his tears increased to a roar.

"I never see him," he sobbed. "I warn't a-nigh the mill at all, and I never see him nor the skiff. Who says I did?"

"What time did you get back to the mill, witness?" asked the coroner.

He didn't know what time it was; his master and missis was come home.

This was true, Mr. Floyd said. They had been back some little time before Ripper showed himself. The first intimation he received of that runagate's presence was when he drew his attention to the loose skiff.

"How came you to see the skiff?" sharply asked the coroner. "Speak up, Ripper."

Ripper spoke up with trembling lips. He was waiting outside after he came up, afraid to go in for fear his master should tan him for not taking the sacks, which they went clean out of his mind, they did, and then he see the little boat; upon which he called out and told his master.

"And it was also you who first saw the body in the water," observed the coroner, regarding the reluctant witness curiously. "How came you to see that? Were you looking for it?"

The witness howled. He didn't know how he come to see it. He was on the strade (estrade), not looking for nothing, when he saw some'at dark among the reeds. He thought it was a big fish a-lodging there, and he told the harvesters when they come by; and they said it was a man, and got him out, and then they found it was the lord.

There was only one peculiarity about the boy's evidence—his manner. All that he said was feasible, quite probable; indeed what would be most likely to happen under the circumstances. But his terror—whence did that arise? Had he been of a timid temperament, it might have been natural; but the miller had spoken the truth—he was audacious and hardy. Only upon one or two, however, did the manner leave any impression. Pike, who made one of the crowd in the inquest-room, was one of these. His experience of human nature was tolerably keen, and he felt sure the boy was keeping something behind that he did not dare to tell. The coroner and jury were not so clear-sighted, and dismissed him with the remark that he was a "little fool."

"Call George Gorton," said the coroner, looking at his notes.

Very much to Lord Hartledon's surprise—perhaps somewhat to his annoyance—the man answering to this name was the one who had originally come to Calne on a special mission to himself. Some feeling caused him to turn from the man while he gave his evidence, as was easy to do in the crowded room.

It appeared that amidst the hubbub and excitement that shook the neighbourhood on the

Tuesday night when the death became known, this stranger happened to avow in the public-house which he made his quarters, that he had seen the Earl of Hartledon in his skiff just before the event must have happened. The information was seized upon, and the man received a summons to appear before the coroner. And it may be as well to remark in this place, what might have been stated earlier, that his second appearance was owing to a little cowardice on his own part. He had felt perfectly satisfied at the time with the promise given him by Lord Hartledon to see the debt paid—given also in the presence of Calne's rector—and took his departure by the train, just as Pike had subsequently told Mr. Elster. But ere he had gone two stages on his journey, he began to think he might have been too precipitate, and to ask himself whether his employers would not tell him so when he appeared before them, unbacked by any guarantee from Lord Hartledon; for this, by a strange oversight, he had omitted to ask for. He halted at once, and went back by the next return-train, forfeiting his third-class fare rather than not remedy the omission. The following day, Tuesday, he spent looking after Lord Hartledon, but, as it happened, did not meet with him.

The man—a dissipated young man, now that his hat was off—came forward in his long coat and with his profusion of red hair and whiskers. But it seemed that he had really very little information to give. He was on the banks of the river when Lord Hartledon passed in the skiff, and noticed how strangely he was rowing, one arm apparently lying useless. He knew nothing at all of any fall his lordship might have had—which, however, he had heard spoken of subsequently— and supposed he was resting his arm from fatigue. What part of the river was this, the coroner asked; and the witness avowed that he could not describe it. He was a stranger, never there but that once; all he knew was that it was higher up, beyond Hartledon House. What might he have been doing there, the keen coroner asked. Only strolling about, was the answer. What was his business at Calne? came the next question; and as it was put the witness caught the eye of the new peer through an opening in the crowd: had it been to save Lord Hartledon's life he could not have helped the signal of caution that unwittingly went out from his eyes, though he would have disdained to use one with his lips. His business, the witness replied to the coroner, was his own business, and did not concern the public, and he respectfully declined to state it. He presumed Calne was a free place like other places, where a stranger might spend a few days without question, if he pleased.

Pike chuckled at this: incipient rebellion to authority warmed that lawless man's heart. He had stood in the shade of the crowd just within the door throughout, attentively watching the witnesses as they gave their evidence: but he was not prepared for what was to come next.

Did the witness see any other spectators on the bank, continued the coroner. Only one, was the answer: a man who was called Pike, or some such name. Pike was watching the little boat on the river when he got up to him: he remarked to

Pike that his lordship's arm seemed tired; and they, he and Pike, had walked back to Calne together.

Pike would have got away had he been able, but the coroner whispered to an officer. For one single moment Mr. Pike seemed inclined to show fight; he began struggling, not gently, to reach the door; the next he gave it up, and resigned himself to his fate. There was a little hubbub, in the midst of which a slip of paper with a pencilled line on it, from Lord Hartledon, was handed to the coroner.

"*Press this point: whether they returned to Calne at once and together.*"

"George Gorton," cried the coroner, as he crushed the paper in his hand, "at what hour did you return to Calne?"

"I went at once. As soon as the little boat was out of sight."

"Went alone?"

"No, sir. I and the man Pike walked together. I've said so already."

"What made you go together?"

"Nothing in particular. We were both going back, I suppose, and strolled along talking."

It appeared to be all that the witness had to tell, and Mr. Pike came forward perforce. As he stood there, his elegant wide-awake bent in his hand, his tawny face dark, his mass of black hair and whiskers and beard all matted and rough, he looked more like the wild man of the woods he had been compared to, than a civilised being. Rough and rude and abrupt were his tones as he spoke, and he bent his face and his eyes—which were light and far sunk, so far as could be seen of them—downwards while he answered. It was in those eyes that the look lay which had struck Mr. Elster as being familiar. He persisted in giving his name as Tom, not Thomas.

But if the stranger man in the long coat had little evidence to give, Pike had even less. He had been in the woods that afternoon, and sauntered out of them to the bank of the river, just as Lord Hartledon passed in the skiff; but he had taken very little notice of him: it was only when the last witness, who came up at the moment, remarked upon the queer manner in which his lordship held his arm, that he saw it was lying down idly.

Not a single thing more could he or would he tell. It was all he knew, he said, and would swear it was all. He went back to Calne with the last witness, and never saw his lordship again alive.

It did appear to be all, just as it did in the matter of the other man. The coroner inquired whether he had seen any one else on the banks or near them, and Pike replied that he had not set eyes on another soul, which Lord Hartledon knew to be false, for he had seen *him*. He was told to put his signature to his evidence, which the clerk had taken down, and he affixed a cross.

"Can't you write?" asked the coroner.

Pike shook his head in the negative. "Never learnt," he curtly said. And my Lord Hartledon, from his place in the room, believed that to be an untruth equally with the other. The earl could not help thinking that the avowal of their going back immediately might be likewise false: it was just as possible that one or other, or both, had followed the course of the boat.

Mr. Carteret was examined. He could tell no more than he had already told: they started together, but he had soon got beyond his lordship, and had never seen him again alive. There was nothing more to be gleaned or gathered. Not the smallest suspicion of foul play, of its being any thing but a pure but most unfortunate accident was entertained for a moment by any one who heard the evidence, and the verdict of the jury was to that effect: Accidental Death.

As the crowd pressed out of the inquest-room, jostling one another in the dusk of the evening, and separated on their several ways, in units or in tens, Lord Hartledon found himself close to Gorton, his coat flapping at his heels as he walked. The man was looking round for Pike: but Mr. Pike, the instant his forced evidence was given, had slunk away from the gaze of his fellow-men, to ensconce himself in his solitary shed. To all appearance Lord Hartledon had overtaken Gorton by accident: the man turned aside in obedience to a signal, and halted. They could not see much of each other's faces in the twilight.

"I wish to ask you a question," said his lordship, in a low, impressive, and not unkindly tone. "Did you speak with my brother, Lord Hartledon, at all on Tuesday?"

"No, my lord, I did not," was the ready answer. "I was trying to get to see his lordship, but did not."

"What did you want with him? What brought you back to Calne?"

"I wanted to get from him a guarantee for— for what your lordship knows of; which he had omitted to give, and I had not thought to ask for," civilly replied the man. "After I left Calne on the Monday night, it struck me I ought to have had something of the sort; and I came back again. I was looking about for his lordship on the Tuesday morning, but did not get to see him. In the afternoon, when the boat-race was over, I made bold to call at Hartledon, but the servants said his lordship wasn't in. As I came away, I saw him, as I thought, pass the lodge and go up the road, and I cut after him, but couldn't overtake him, and at last lost sight of him. I struck into a tangled sort of path through the gorse, or what it's called down here, and it brought me out near the river. His lordship was just passing down it in the sculler-boat, and then I knew it was somebody else that had gone by the lodge, and not him. Perhaps it was your lordship?"

"You knew it was Lord Hartledon in the boat? I mean, you recognised him? You did not mistake him for me?"

"I knew him for himself, my lord. If I'd been a bit nearer the lodge, I shouldn't have been likely to mistake even your lordship for him."

Lord Hartledon was gazing into the man's face still; never once had his eyes been removed from it.

"You did not see Lord Hartledon later?"

"I never saw him all day but that once when he passed in the skiff. I—"

"You did not follow him, then?"

"Where'd have been the use of that?" debated the man. "I couldn't call out my business from the banks, and I didn't know his lordship was going to land lower down. I went straight back to Calne, my lord, walking with that man Pike —who is a rum fellow, and has got a history behind him, unless I'm mistaken; but it's no business of mine. I made my mind up to another night on't in Calne, thinking I'd get to Hartledon early the next morning before his lordship had time to go out; and I was sitting comfortable with a pipe and a drop of beer, when news came of the accident."

Lord Hartledon believed the man to be telling the strict truth; and a weight—whose source he did not stay to analyse—lifted itself off his mind. But he asked another question.

" Why are you in Calne still?"

" I waited for orders. After his lordship died I couldn't go away without 'em—carrying with me nothing but the word of a dead man. The orders came this morning, safe enough; but I had got the summons served on me then to attend the inquest, and had to stay for it. I'm going away now, my lord, by the first train."

Lord Hartledon was satisfied, and nodded his head. As he turned back he met Dr. Ashton.

"I was looking for you, Lord Hartledon. If you require any assistance or information in the various arrangements and business that now devolve upon you, I shall be happy to render both. There will be a good deal to do in one way or another; more than, I daresay, your inexperience has the least notion of. You will have your solicitor at hand, of course; but if you want me, you know where to find me."

The rector's words were courteous, but the tone was not a warm one, and the title "Lord Hartledon" grated on Val's ear. In his impulse he grasped the speaker's hand, pouring forth a heart's prayer.

"O Dr. Ashton, will you not forgive me? The horrible trouble I brought upon myself is over now. I don't rejoice in it under the circumstances, heaven knows; I only speak of the fact. Let me come to your house again! Forgive me for the past."

"In one sense the trouble is over, because the

debts that were a formidable embarrassment to Mr. Elster are as nothing to Lord Hartledon," was the reply. "But let me assure you of one thing: that your being the Earl of Hartledon will not make the slightest difference to my decision not to give you my daughter, unless your line of conduct shall change."

"It is changed. Dr. Ashton, on my word of honour, I will never be guilty of carelessness again. One thing will be my safeguard, though all else should fail—the fact that I passed my word for this to my dear brother not many hours before his death. For my sake, for Anne's sake, you'll forgive me!"

Was it possible to resist the persuasive tone, the clear earnestness of the dark-blue honest eyes? If ever Percival Elster was to make an effort for good, and succeed, it must be now. The doctor knew it; and he knew that Anne's happiness was at stake! But he did not thaw immediately.

"You know, Lord Hartledon—"

"Call me Val, as you used to do," came the

pleading interruption; and Dr. Ashton smiled in spite of himself.

"Percival, you know that it is against my nature to be harsh, or to be unforgiving; just as I believe it is contrary to your nature to be guilty of deliberate wrong. If you will only be true to yourself, I would rather have you for my son-in-law than any other man in England; as I would have had when you were Val Elster. Do you note my words: *true to yourself*."

"As I will be from henceforth," whispered Val, the tears of earnestness rising in his eyes.

And as he would have been but for his besetting sin—vacillation.

CHAPTER XII.

MR. PIKE'S WHISPER TO JABEZ GUM.

It happened that Clerk Gum had some business on hand the day of the inquest, which obliged him to go to Garchester. He reached home after dark; and the first thing he saw was his wife, in what he was pleased to call a state of semi-idiotcy. The tea-things were laid on the table, some substantial refreshment in the shape of cold meat, and a plate of muffins ready for toasting, all for the clerk's regalement. But Mrs. Gum herself sat on a low chair by the fire, her cap in disorder, her straw-coloured hair all awry, and her eyes swollen with crying.

"What's the matter now?" was the clerk's first question.

"O Gum! I told you you ought not to have went off to-day. You might have stayed to be at the inquest."

"Much good I should do the inquest, or the inquest me," retorted the clerk. "Is Becca gone?"

"Long ago. Gum, that dream's coming round. I said it would. I *told* you there was ill boding to Lord Hartledon; and that Pike was mixed up in it, and Mr. Elster also in some way. If you'd only listened to me—"

The clerk, who had been brushing his hat and shaking the dust from his outer-coat—for he was a very careful man with his clothes, and was always dressed well—brought down his hand upon the table with some temper.

"Just you stop that. I've heard enough of that dream, and of all your dreams. Confounded folly! Haven't I trouble and worry enough upon my mind, without your worrying me every time I come in about your idiotic dreams?"

"Well," returned Mrs. Gum rather sullenly, "if the dream's nothing, I'd like to ask why they had Pike up to-day afore 'em all?"

"Who had him up?" asked the clerk, after a pause. "Had him up where?"

"Afore the law-people that were sitting on the body of Lord Hartledon: afore the new lord, afore Dr. Ashton, afore all the constables and police the place contains—afore every body," ran on Mrs. Gum. "Lydda Jones brought me the news just now. 'So they had Pike the poacher up,' says she. 'He was took up afore the jury, and them, and had to confess to't.' 'Confess to what?' says I. 'Why, that he was about in the woods up there when my lord met his end,' says she; 'and it's to know how my lord *did* meet it, and whether the poacher mightn't have dealt out that blow he had on his temple and robbed him after it.' Gum, I've sat here since a-twittering and a-quaking—"

"There's no suspicion of any foul play—that his lordship's death was not an accident, is there?" questioned the clerk, in a strangely-subdued tone of fear.

"Not that I know of, except in Lydda's cranky temper," answered Mrs. Gum. "But I don't like to hear he was up there. And when I think of my dream—"

"Drat your dream!" angrily apostrophised

Mr. Gum. "That Lydda Jones is a foul-tongued woman, capable of swearing away any man's life. Is Pike in custody?"

"Not yet. They've let him off for the present—leastways Lydda said so. O Gum, often and often do I wish my days was ended!"

"Often and often do I wish I'd a quiet house to come into, and not be bothered with dreams," was the scornful retort of Mrs. Gum's lord. "Suppose you toast them muffins?"

She gave a sigh or two, put her cap straight on her ragged hair, and meekly arose to obey. The clerk was carefully folding up the outer coat, for it was one he only wore on high-days, when he felt something in the pocket—a small parcel.

"I'd a'most forgotten this," he exclaimed, taking it out. "Thanks to you, Nance Gum! What with your dreams, and your other worryings, I can't think of my proper business."

"What is it?" she asked, looking round at the parcel.

"It's a deed that Dr. Ashton's lawyer got me to bring and save his clerk a journey—if you must know. I'll take it over at once, while the tea's brewing."

"Pike can't write," exclaimed Mrs. Gum, rather inopportunely recurring to the past subject, as she cut a muffin in two.

"Can't write?"

"Lydda says so. When he was wanted to swear to the truth of what he'd said, by signing his name, he made a cross, and told 'em he'd never learnt writing."

"Get on with them muffins," was the rejoinder. "Standing gaping, with the fork in one hand and the muffin in t'other, won't toast 'em."

As Jabez Gum passed through his own gate he looked towards the dwelling-place of Mr. Pike; it was only natural he should after the recent conversation; and he saw that worthy gentleman come stealing from it across the waste ground, with his usual cautious step. Although not given to seek an interchange of courtesies with his neighbour, the clerk walked briskly towards him now, and waited at the hurdles which divided the waste ground from the road.

"I hear you were prowling about the mill when Lord Hartledon met with his accident," began the clerk in a condemning but very low tone.

"And what if I was?" asked Pike, leaning his arms on the hurdles, and facing the clerk while he answered. "Near the mill I wasn't; about the woods and the river I was; and I saw him pass down in the sculler-boat with his disabled arm. What of it, I ask?"

Pike's tone, though short, was civil enough. The forced appearance before the coroner and public that day had disturbed his inward equanimity in no slight degree, and taken for the present all insolence out of him.

"Should any doubt get afloat that his lordship's death might not have been accidental, your presence at the spot would tell against you."

"No, it wouldn't. I left the spot afore the accident could have happened; as soon as he had passed the round trees—for that's where I was, and no higher; and I came back to Calne along with a witness. As to the death having been something worse than accident, there's not a soul in the place has dreamt of such a thing, except me."

"Except you! What do you mean?"

Pike, whose legs and feet were hidden behind the low hedge, leaned more forward over the hurdles, so as to bring his disreputable face close to the respectable one of Mr. Gum. The clerk slightly recoiled; not far, or he could not have caught the low whisper.

"I don't think the death was accidental. I believe his lordship was just put out of the way quietly."

"Heaven forbid!" exclaimed the shocked clerk. "By whom? By you?" he added in his bewilderment.

"No," returned the man, with the cool equanimity of one who is certain of his own ground. "If I'd done it, I shouldn't talk of it."

"What do you mean?" cried Mr. Gum.

"I mean that I have my suspicions; and good suspicions they are. Many a man has been hung on less. I am not going to tell of 'em; perhaps not ever. I shall wait and keep my eyes open, and bring 'em, if I can, into certainties. Time enough to talk then, or to hush 'em for good, as circumstances may prompt."

"And you tell me you were not near the place at the time of the accident?"

"*I* wasn't," replied Mr. Pike, with emphasis.

"Who was?"

"That's my secret. And as I've got a little matter of business on hand to-night, I don't care to be further delayed, if it's all the same to you, neighbour. And instead of your accusing me of prowling about the mill again, perhaps you'll just give a thought occasional to what I have now said, keeping it to yourself. I'm not afraid of your spreading it in Calne; for it might bring a hornet's nest about your head, and about some other heads that you'd not like to see stung."

With the last words Mr. Pike crossed the hurdles and went off in the direction of Hartledon. It was a light night, and the clerk stood and stared after him. To say [that Mr. Jabez Gum in his astonishment was uncertain, metaphorically speaking, whether he stood on his head or his heels, would be saying little; and how much of these assertions he might believe, and whether he had not fatally compromised his dignity by holding converse with this strange man in the public road, and what mischief Mr. Pike might be going after to-night, he knew not. Drawing a long sigh, which did not sound very much like a sigh of relief, he at length turned off to Dr. Ashton's, and the man disappeared.

We must follow Pike. He went stealthily up the road past Hartledon, keeping under the shade of the hedge, and shrinking right into it when he saw any body coming. Striking off when he got near the mill, he approached it cautiously, and halted amidst some side trees, whence he had a view of the mill-door.

He was waiting for the boy, John Ripper. Fully convinced by the lad's manner at the inquest that he had not told all he knew, but was keeping something back in fear, Mr. Pike, for reasons of his own, resolved to come at it if he could. He knew that the boy would be at work later than usual that night, having been hindered in the afternoon.

Imagine yourself standing with your back to the river, reader—that is, to this arm of it—and take a view of the premises as they face you. The cottage is a square building, and has four good rooms on the ground-floor: a kitchen and a parlour in front, two sleeping-rooms at the back. With the back we have nothing to do. The miller's thrifty and careful wife generally locked all these rooms up if she went out, and carried the keys away in her pocket; possibly as an additional precaution against thieves. The parlour-window was an ordinary sash-window, with outside shutters; the kitchen-window was a small casement-window, opening inside, and was protected outside by a fixed net-work of wire. Nobody could get in or out, even when the casement was open, without tearing this wire away, which would not be a difficult matter to accomplish. On the left of the cottage, but to your right as you face it, stands the mill, to which you ascend by steps. It communicates inside with the upper floor of the cottage, which is used as a store-room for corn; and from this store-room a flight of stairs descends to the kitchen below, shut in by a black door in the corner, near the eight-day clock. There is also another flight of stairs from this store-room, which communicates with the open passage leading from the back door to the stable. This is all that need be said: and you may think it superfluous to have said it at all: but it is not.

Master Ripper came forth at length. With a shuddering avoidance of the water—which Mr. Pike did not fail to detect with his practised eyes, accustomed to the dark more than the light—he came tearing along like one running from a ghost, and was darting past the trees, when he found himself made a prisoner by a detaining arm of great strength. Mr. Pike clapped his other hand upon the boy's mouth, stifling a howl of terror in the bud.

"Do you see this, young Rip?" cried he.

Rip did see it. It was a pistol with a bright barrel, and was held rather inconveniently close to the young man's breast. Rip loved his life dearly; but it nearly went out of him then with fear.

"Now," said Pike, "I'm come up to know about this business of Lord Hartledon's, and I will know it, or else I'll leave you as dead as he is. And I'll have you took up for murder into the bargain," he rather illogically continued, "as an accessory to the fact."

David Ripper was in a bath of horror; all idea of concealment gone out of him. "I couldn't help it," he gasped. "I couldn't get out to him; I was locked up in the mill. Don't shoot me."

"I think I will," deliberated Mr. Pike aloud; and young Rip felt his hair rise on end in his agony of sickness.

"I'll spare you on one condition," decided Mr. Pike. "You disclose the whole of this from the top to the tail, and then maybe we shall part friends. But you only stick at one jot, or try to palm off one lie, and I'll riddle you through. To begin with: what brought you locked up in the mill?"

It was a wicked tale of a wicked young jail-bird, as Mr. Pike (probably the worst jail-bird by far of the two) phrased it. Master Ripper had purposely caused himself to be locked in the mill, his object being to supply himself with as much corn as he could stuff in his pockets or carry about him in any way for the benefit of his rabbits and pigeons, and other live stock at home. He had done it twice before, he avowed, in mortal dread of the proximate pistol, and had got away all safe through the square hole in the passage at foot of the back staircase, whence he had dropped to the ground. To his consternation on this occasion, however, he had found the door at the foot of the stairs bolted, as it never had been before, and he could not get to the passage. So that he was a prisoner all the afternoon, and had exercised his legs as much as he pleased between the store-room and the kitchen, both of which were open to him.

If ever a man showed virtuous indignation at a sinner's confession, Mr. Pike showed it now, and the pistol shook ominously. "That's how you were about in the stubble-field a-setting your trap, you young villain! I saw the coroner look at you. And now about Lord Hartledon. What did you see?"

Master Ripper rubbed the perspiration from his face, as he went on with his tale; but the more he rubbed the worse it got again. Pike listened with all the ears he possessed, and more than the eyes—listened and said not a word, beyond a "get on," and sundry rough reminders of that nature, until the tale was done.

"You awful young dog! You saw all that from the kitchen-window, and never tried to get out of it!"

"I *couldn't* get out of it," pleaded the boy in his agony. "It have got a wire-net afore it, that winder have. I couldn't break that."

"You are strong enough to break it ten times over," retorted Pike.

"But then master and missis 'ud ha' knowed I'd been in the mill!" cried the boy, a gleam of cunning showing through the terror of his eyes.

"Ugh," grunted Pike. "And you saw exactly what you've told me?"

"I see it for sure, and I heard the cries."

"Did he see you?"

"No; I were afeard to show myself. And the boat weren't right off the winder; 'twere yards to the side on't. When master come home, the first thing he did was t' unlock that there staircase-door, and I got out without his seeing me——"

"Where did you hide the grain your pockets were loaded with?" demanded Pike.

"I'd emptied of it out again in the store-room," returned the boy, gloomily. "I telled master there were a loose skiff out there," he added, in pursuance of his narrative, "and he come out and secured it. Them harvesters come up next and got him out of the water."

"Yes, you could see fast enough what you were looking for! Well, young Rip," continued Mr. Pike, consolingly, "you stand about as rich a chance of being took up for a hempen dance in the air as ever you'll stand in all your born days, with decent luck. If you'd jumped through that wire, you'd have saved the lord, and he'd have made it right for you with old Floyd. I'd advise you to keep a silent tongue in your head always, if you want to save your neck."

"I was a-keeping of it, till you come and made me tell with that there pistol," howled the boy.

"And particularly lucky you may count yourself that you did tell, and have not got its contents inside of you," returned Mr. Pike.

"You won't go and split on me?" asked the boy, with shivering lips.

"I won't split on you about the grain at all," graciously promised Mr. Pike. "If you get yourself locked in daily to lighten the granary, it's no business of mine. The miller might make it his perhaps, but that's his look-out and yours. As to the other matter—well, I'll not say any thing about that; leastways, yet awhile. You keep it a secret; so'll I."

With a flourish of the pistol, but without another word, Mr. Pike extended his hand as a signal that the culprit was at liberty to depart;

and he scuttered off as fast as his legs would carry him. Pike then returned the pistol to his pocket— in a very careless manner, if it had any thing in it —and took his way back to Calne in a thoughtful mood, and a particularly ungenial one. There was a doubt within him whether the boy had disclosed the truth, even to him.

Perhaps on no one—with the exception of the new peer—did the death of Lord Hartledon tell home as it did on Lady Kirton and her daughter Maude. To the one it brought embarrassment; to the other, what seemed very like a broken heart. The Countess Dowager's tactics must change as by magic. She had to transfer the affection and consideration evinced for Edward Lord Hartledon to his brother Percival; and to do it easily and naturally. She had to obliterate from the latter's mind her overbearing dislike to him, to cause her insults to be remembered no more. A difficult task, even for her, wily woman as she was.

How was it to be done? For three mortal hours, the night after Lord Hartledon's death, did she lie awake, thinking of her plans; perhaps for the first time in her life, for obtuse natures don't lie awake. The death had not affected her, except in regard to her own interests; she could feel for none and regret none in her utter selfishness. One was fallen, but another had risen. "Le roi est mort: vive le roi!"

On the day following the death, she had sought an interview with Percival. Never a woman evinced better tact in an interview than she in that. There was no violent change in her manner, no apologies for the past, or display of sudden-born affection. She spoke quietly and sensibly with him of passing topics: the death, and what could have led to it; the immediate business on hand, some of the changes it entailed for the future. "I'll stop with you still, Percival," she said, "and look after things a bit for you, as I have been doing for your brother. It is an awful shock, and we must all have time to get over it. Ah me! if I had only foreseen this, how I might have spared my temper and my poor Maude's feelings!"

She looked sideways with the corner of her eye

at the young earl; but he evinced no curiosity to hear more, so she went on unasked.

"You know, Val, for a portionless girl, as Maude is, it was a great blow to me when I found her fixing her heart upon a younger son. How cross and unjust it made me I couldn't conceal: mothers are mothers. I wanted her to take a fancy to Hartledon, dear fellow, and I suppose she could not, and it rendered me cross; and I know I worried her and worried my own temper, till at times I was not conscious what I said. Poor Maude! she did not rebel openly, but I could see the struggle in her tender bosom. Only a week ago, when Hartledon was talking to her about his marrying sometime, and hinting that she might care for him if she tried, she scored her beautiful drawing all over with ugly marks; jobbed the pencil through it——"

"But why do you tell me this now?" asked Val.

"Hartledon—dear me! I wonder how long I shall be getting accustomed to your name?— there's only you and me and Maude left now of the family," cried the Dowager impressively, peering at him from beneath her flaxen front, which had dropped on to her eyebrows; "and if I speak of such things, it is in the fulness of my heart. And now about these letters: do you care how they are worded?"

"I don't seem to care about any thing," listlessly answered the young man. "As to the letters, I think I'd rather write them myself, Lady Kirton."

"Indeed no, you shall not have trouble thrust upon you to-day. *I'*ll write the letters, and do you indulge yourself by doing nothing."

He yielded to her in his unstable nature. They were business letters that she spoke of, and it was more suitable that he should write them; he wished to write them; but she carried her point, and merged his will in hers. Would it be a type of the future?—would he yield to her in other things as he was yielding now, in defiance of his better judgment? Alas! alas!

She picked up her skirts and left him, and went sailing up stairs to her daughter's room.

Maude was sitting shivering in a shawl, though the day was hot.

"I've paved the way," nodded the old woman, in a meaning tone. "And there's one fortunate thing about Val: he is so truthful himself, so ultra-honourable, that he can't see deceit or suspect it. One may take him in with his eyes open."

Maude turned *her* eyes upon her mother. Very languid and unspeculative eyes they were just then.

"I gave him a hint, Maude, that you had been unable to bring yourself to like Hartledon, but had fixed your mind on a younger son. Later we'll let him suspect who the younger son was."

The words aroused Maude; she started up in her chair, and stood staring at her mother, her eyes dilating with a sort of horror; her pale cheeks slowly turning to crimson.

"I don't understand," she gasped; "I *hope* I don't understand. You—you do not mean that I am to try to like Val Elster?"

"Now, Maude, no heroics. I'll not see *you* make a fool of yourself as your sisters have done. He's not Val Elster any longer; he is the Earl of Hartledon: and he's better-looking than ever his brother was, and he'll make a better husband, for he'll be more easily led."

"I would not marry Val for the whole world," she said, catching up her breath with emotion. "I dislike him; I hate him; I never could be a wife to Val Elster."

"We'll see," said the Dowager, pushing up her front, of which she had just caught a sight in a glass.

"Thank Heaven, there's no fear of it!" resumed Maude, collecting her senses, and sitting down again with a relieved sigh; "he is to marry Anne Ashton. Thank Heaven that he loves her!"

"Anne Ashton!" scornfully returned the Countess Dowager. "She might have been tolerated when he was Val Elster, not now he is Earl of Hartledon. What notions you have, Maude!"

Maude burst into tears. "Mamma, I think it is fearfully indecent for you to begin upon these things already! It only happened last night, and —and it sounds quite horrible."

"When one has to look out for one's living, one has to do many things decent and indecent," retorted the Countess Dowager in a sharp tone. "He has got his hint, and you've got yours: and you are no true girl if you suffer yourself now to be triumphed over by Anne Ashton."

Maude cried on silently. She was thinking how cruel fate was to have taken the one brother and spared the other. Who—save that Anne Ashton—would have missed Val Elster; while Lord Hartledon—at least he had made the life of one heart. A poor bruised heart now; never, never to be made quite whole again.

Thus the Countess Dowager, in her blindness, began her plans. In her blindness! If we could but foresee the ending of some of the unholy schemes that many of us are apt to weave, we might be more content to leave them humbly in a higher Hand. Do they ever bring good, these plans, born of our evil passions; hatred, malice, utter selfishness? I think not. They may seem to succeed triumphantly, but—watch the trumph to the end.

CHAPTER XIII.

PITCH-POTS BURNING.

THE dews of an October evening, following on a fine day, were arising in Calne, as Lord Hartledon walked along from the railway station. Just as unexpectedly as he had arrived the morning you first saw him, when he was only Val Elster, had he arrived now. By the merest accident one of the Hartledon servants happened to be at the station when the train arrived, and he took charge of his master's luggage.

"All well at home, James?'

"All quite well, my lord."

Several weeks had elapsed since his brother's death, and Lord Hartledon had spent them in London. He went up on business the week after the funeral, and did not return again. In one respect he had no inducement to return; for the

Ashton family, including Anne, were on a visit in Wales. They were at home now, as he knew full well: perhaps that had brought him down.

He went in unannounced, finding his way to the inner drawing-room. A large fire blazed in the grate, and the Lady Maude sat by it so intent in thought as not to observe his entrance. She wore a black crape dress, with a little white trimming on its low body and sleeves. The firelight played on her beautiful features, and her eyelashes glistened as if with tears: she was thinner and paler; he saw it at once. The Countess Dowager stuck to Hartledon like a leech, and evinced no intention of moving away from it: she and her daughter had been there alone all these weeks.

"How are you, Maude?"

She looked round and started up with a scream, backing from him with a face of alarm. Ah, was it *instinct* caused her so to back? What, or who, was she thinking of; holding her hands before her with that face of horror?

"Surely, Maude, you know me!"

"Percival! I beg your pardon. I believe I was thinking of — of your brother, and I really did not know you in the uncertain light. We are not on company manners, and don't get our rooms lighted early," she added with a little laugh.

He took her hands in his. Now that she knew him, and the alarm was over, she seemed really pleased to see him: the dark eyes were raised to his with a frank smile of gladness.

"May I take a cousin's kiss of greeting, Maude?"

Without waiting for yes or no, he stooped and took it. Maude flung his hands away. He should have left out the word "cousin," or not have taken the kiss.

He went and stood with his elbow on the mantel-piece, soberly, as if he had but kissed a sister. Maude sat down again.

"Why did you not send us word you were coming?" she asked.

"There was no necessity for it. And I only made my mind up this morning."

"What a long while you have been away! I thought you went for a week."

"I did not get my business over very quickly; and afterwards I waited to see Thomas Carr: he was out of town. The Ashtons were away, you know; so I had no inducement to hurry back."

"Very complimentary to *her*. Who's Thomas Carr?" asked Lady Maude.

"The greatest friend I possess in this world. He is a barrister. We were at college together, and he used to keep me straight."

"Keep you straight! Val!"

"It's true. I went to him in all my scrapes and troubles. He is the most honourable, upright, straightforward man I know; and, as such, possesses a talent for serving—"

"Hartledon! Is it *you*?"

The interruption came from the Countess Dowager. She and the butler came in together, both looking equally astonished at sight of the earl. The former said the dinner was served.

"Will you let me sit down in this coat?" asked Val.

The Countess Dowager would willingly have allowed him to sit down without any. Her welcome was demonstrative; her displayed affection already warm, and she called him "Val" tenderly. He escaped for a minute to his room, washed his hands, gave his hair a brush, and was down again, and taking the head of his own table.

It was something pleasant to have him there— a welcome change from Hartledon's recent monotony; and even Lady Maude, with her boasted dislike, felt prejudice melting away. Boasted dislike it had been, not real. None could dislike Percival He was not Edward Lord Hartledon, and it was him Maude had loved. Percival she never would love, but she might learn to like him. As he sat there near her, in his plain black morning attire, courteously kind, genuinely sweet-tempered, his good looks all conspicuous, a smile on his delicate, his refined, but his vacillating lips, and his dark-blue honest eyes bent upon her in single-hearted kindness, Maude for the first time admitted a vision of the possible future, together with a dim consciousness that it might not be intolerable.

Half the world, of her age and sex, would have deemed it indeed a triumph to be made the wife of that attractive man.

He had courteously stood aside for Lady Kirton to take the head of the table; but the Dowager had positively refused, and subsided into the chair at the foot. She did not fill it in dear Edward's time, she said; neither should she in dear Val's; he had come home to occupy his place as Hartledon's lord. And O, thank goodness that he was come! she added, turning up the whites of her eyes: she and Maude had been so lonely and miserable, losing flesh daily from sheer ennui. So she faced Lord Hartledon at the end of the table, her flaxen curls surmounted by an array of black plumes, and looking very much like a stout female mute.

"What an awful thing this is about the rectory!" exclaimed she, speaking with her mouth full of high-seasoned maccaroni, when they were pretty well through the dinner — and it may be remarked, that she liked all her dishes high-seasoned.

Lord Hartledon looked up quietly, "What is the matter at the rectory?"

"They have got a fever broken out."

"Is that all!" he exclaimed, some amusement on his face. "I thought it must have taken fire."

"A fever's worse than a fire."

"Do you think so?"

"*Think so!*" echoed the Countess Dowager, opening her round eyes. "You can run away from a fire; but a fever may take hold of you before you are aware of it. Every soul in the rectory may die; it may spread to the parish; it may spread here. I have caused tar to be kept burning round the house the last two days."

"You are not serious, Lady Kirton!"

"I am serious. I'd not catch a fever for the whole world. I should die of fright, before it had time to kill me of itself. Besides—I have Maude to guard. You were forgetting her."

"There's no danger at all. One of the servants became ill after they returned home, and it proved to be a fever. I don't suppose it will spread."

"How did *you* hear about it?"

"From Miss Ashton. She mentioned it in her last letter to me."

"I didn't know you corresponded with her," cried the Dowager, her tone rather shrill.

"Not correspond with Miss Ashton!" he repeated. "Of course I do."

The old Dowager had a fit of choking: some maccaroni went the wrong way, she said. The earl resumed.

"It is an awful shame of those seaside lodging-house people! Did you hear the particulars, Maude? After the Ashtons concluded their visit in Wales, they went for a fortnight to the seaside, on their way home, taking lodgings. Some days after they had been settled in the apartments they discovered that some fever was in the house; a family who occupied another set of apartments being ill with it, and had been ill before the Ashtons went in. Dr. Ashton told the landlady what he thought of her conduct, and then they quitted the house for home. But Mrs. Ashton's maid, Matilda, had already taken it."

"Did Miss Ashton give you these particulars?" asked Lady Maude, toying with a late rose that lay beside her plate.

"Yes. I should feel inclined to prosecute the woman, were I Dr. Ashton, for having been so selfishly inconsiderate. But I hope Matilda is better, and that the alarm will end with her. It is four days since I had Anne's letter."

"Then, Lord Hartledon, I can tell you that the alarm's worse, and another has taken it, and the parish is up in arms," spoke the Countess Dowager tartly. "It has proved to be a fever of a most malignant type, and not a soul but Hillary the surgeon goes near the rectory. You must not venture within half a mile of it. Dr. Ashton was so careless as to occupy his pulpit on Sunday; but thank goodness I did not venture to church, or allow Maude to go. Your Miss Ashton will be having it next."

"Of course they have advice from Garchester?" he exclaimed.

"How should I know? My opinion is that the parson himself might be prosecuted for bringing the fever into a healthy neighbourhood. Now, Hedges, some port! One has need to take a double portion of tonics to fortify oneself in a time like this."

The Countess Dowager's alarms were not feigned—no, nor exaggerated; but real. She had an intense, selfish fear of any sort of illness; she had a worse fear of death. In any time of public epidemic her displayed terrors of it would have been almost ludicrous in their absurdity, but that they were so real. And she "fortified" herself against infection by eating and drinking more than ever.

Nothing else was said: she shunned allusion to it when she could; and presently she and Maude quitted the dining-room. "You won't be long, Hartledon?" she observed sweetly, as she passed him. Val only bowed in answer, closed the door upon them, and rang the bell for Hedges.

"Is much alarm excited in regard to this fever at the rectory?" he asked of the butler.

"Not very much, I think, my lord. A few are timid about it; as is always the case. One of the other servants has taken it; but Mr. Hillary told me when he was here this morning that he hoped it would not spread beyond the rectory."

"Was Hillary here this morning? Nobody's ill?" asked Lord Hartledon quickly.

"No one at all, my lord. The Countess Dowager sent for him, to ask what her diet had better be, and how she could guard against infection more effectually than she was doing. She did not allow him to come in, but spoke to him from one of the upper windows with a cloak and respirator on."

Lord Hartledon looked at his butler; the man was suppressing a grim smile.

"Nonsense, Hedges!"

"It's true, my lord. Mrs. Mirrable says she has got five saucers of lime inside their rooms, and an earthen pot of pitch burning."

Lord Hartledon broke into a laugh, not suppressed.

"And in the side courtyard, which looks towards the rectory, as may be said, there's ever so many pitch-pots alight night and day," added Hedges. "We have had five hundred people up, wanting to know if the place is on fire."

"What a joke!" cried his lordship — who was not beyond the age yet to enjoy such jokes. "Hedges," he resumed, changing his tone to a more confidential one, "no strangers have been here inquiring for me, I suppose?"

He alluded to creditors, or people acting for them. To a careless man, as Val had been, it was a difficult matter to know whether all his debts were paid or not. He had settled what he remembered; but there might be others. Hedges understood; and his voice dropped to the same low tone: he had been pretty cognisant of the embarrassments of the Honourable Mr. Elster.

"Nobody at all, my lord. They'd not have got much information out of me, if they had come."

Lord Hartledon laughed. "Things are changed now, Hedges, and they may get as much information as they choose. Bring me a cup of coffee here; make haste."

The coffee was brought, and he went out as soon as he had drank it, taking the road to the rectory. It was a calm still night, the moon tolerably bright; not a breath of wind stirred the air; warm and oppressive for October: not by any means the sort of night that doctors covet when fever's in the atmosphere.

He turned in at the rectory-gates, and was crossing to the house, when a flutter of leaves in a side-shrubbery path caused him to look over the dwarf laurels, and he saw Anne. He was at her side in an instant. She was without her bonnet, as if she had just come forth from the rooms for a breath of air. As was indeed the case.

"My darling!"

"I heard you had come," she whispered, as he held both her hands in his, and her heart bounded with an exquisite flutter of delight.

"How did you hear that?" he asked, placing her hand within his arm, that he might pace the walk with her.

"Papa heard it. Some one had seen you

walking home from the train: I think it was Mr. Hillary. But, Percival, ought you to have come here?" she added, stopping in alarm. "This is infected ground, you know."

"Not for me. I have no more fear of catching a fever than I have of catching a moonstroke. Anne, I hope *you* will not take it," he gravely added.

"I hope not, either. Like you, I have no fear of it. I am so glad Arthur is away. Was it not wrong of that landlady to let her apartments to us when she had fever in them?"

"It was infamously wrong," said Lord Hartledon warmly.

"She excused herself afterwards by saying, that as the people who had the fever were in quite a different part of the house from that she let to us, she thought there could be no danger. Papa was so angry. He told her he was sorry the law did not take cognisance of such an offence. We had been a week in the house before we knew of it."

"How did you find it out?"

"The lady who was ill with it died, and

Matilda saw the coffin—a shell they called it—going up the back stairs. She questioned the servants of the house, and one of them told her all about it then, bit by bit. Another lady was lying ill, and a third was getting well. The landlady, by way of excusing herself, said that the greatest wrong had been done to herself, for these ladies had brought the fever into her house, and brought it deliberately. Fever had broken out in their own home, some long way off, and they ran away from it, and took her apartments, saying nothing; which was true, we found."

"Two wrongs don't make a right," observed Lord Hartledon. "Their bringing the fever surreptitiously into her house was no justification for her receiving you into it when it was there. It's the way of the world, Anne: one wrong leading to many. Is Matilda getting over it?"

"I hardly know. She is not out of danger; but Mr. Hillary has hopes of her. One of the other servants has taken it, and is worse than Matilda. Mr. Hillary has been with her three times to-day, and is coming again. She was ill when I last wrote to you, Val; but we did not know it."

"Which of them is it?" he asked.

"It's the dairy-maid. I don't suppose you know her. She is a big, stout, full-bodied girl, and has never had a day's illness before. There was some trouble with her. She would not take any medicine; would not lie by; would not, in short, do any thing that she ought to have done, and the consequence is that the fever has got dangerously ahead. I am sure she is very ill."

"I hope it will not spread beyond the rectory."

"O Val, that is our one great hope," she said, her earnest face brightening with its own hope, as she turned it to him in the moonlight. "We are taking all the precautions against it that we can take. None of us are going abroad beyond the grounds, except papa, and we do not welcome any body here. I don't know what papa will say to your coming."

He smiled. "But you can't keep all the world away!"

"We do—nearly. Mr. Hillary comes, and

Dr. Beamish from Garchester, and one or two people have been here on business. If any body calls at the gate, they are not asked in; and I don't suppose they would come in if asked. Jabez Gum's the most obstinate. He comes in just as usual, and will come. 'As if such a thing as fever would touch me, Miss Anne!' he said to me this morning. 'My body's too genteel for it.' It made me laugh."

"Lady Kirton, up at Hartledon, is in an awful fright," said Val; his tone one of amusement instead of commiseration.

"O, I have heard of it," cried Anne, clasping her hands in laughter. "She is burning tar-barrels outside the house; and she spoke to Mr. Hillary this morning through the window, muffled up in a cloak and blue respirator. What a strange old thing she is!"

Val shrugged his shoulders. "I don't think she's bad-meaning au fond; and she has no home, poor creature."

"Is that why she remains so long at Hartledon?"

"I suppose so. The reigning at Hartledon must be something like a glimpse of Paradise to her. She'll not quit it in a hurry."

"I wonder you like her to be there."

"I know I shall never have courage to tell her to go," was the candid and characteristic answer. "I was afraid of her as a boy, and I'm not sure but I'm afraid still."

"I don't like her—I don't like either of them," said Anne, in a low tone.

Lord Hartledon twitched a sprig of box from the shrubbery hedge as he passed. "Don't you like Maude?"

"No. I am sure she is not true. To my mind there is something very false about them both."

"I think you are wrong, Anne; certainly so as regards Maude."

Miss Ashton did not press her opinion: they were his relatives. "But I should have pitied poor Edward had he lived and married her," she said, following out her thoughts.

"I was mistaken when I thought Maude cared

for Edward," observed Lord Hartledon. "I'm sure I did think it. I used to tell Edward so; but a day or two after he died, I found I was wrong. The Dowager had been urging Maude to like him, and she could not, and it made her miserable."

"Did Maude tell you this?" inquired Anne; her radiant eyes full of surprise as they were turned upon the earl.

"Not Maude: she never said a word to me upon the subject. It was the countess."

"Then, Val, she must have said it to you with an object: I am sure Maude did love him. I know she did."

He shook his head. "You are wrong, Anne, depend upon it. She did not like him, and she and her mother were at variance upon the point. However, it is of no moment to discuss it now: and it might never have come to an issue had Edward lived, for he did not care for her: and I daresay never would have cared for her."

Anne said no more. It was of no moment, as he observed; but she retained her own opinion.

They walked from one end to the other of the short walk in silence, and Anne said she must go in.

"Am I quite forgiven?" whispered Lord Hartledon, bending his head down to her.

"I never thought I had very much to forgive," she rejoined, after a pause.

"My darling! I mean by your father."

"Ah, I don't know. You must talk to him. He knows we have been writing to each other. I think he means to trust you."

"The best plan will be for you to come soon to Hartledon, Anne. I shall never go wrong when once you are my wife."

"Do you go so very wrong now?" she asked.

"On my honour, no! You need not doubt me, Anne; now or ever. I have paid up what I owed, and will take very good care to keep out of trouble for the future. I incurred the debts for others, more than for myself, and I have bought experience dearly. My darling, surely you can trust me now?"

"I always did trust you," she murmured.

He took a long, fervent kiss from her lips, and then led her to the open lawn and across to the house.

"Ought you to come in, Percival?"

"Certainly. One word, Anne; because I may be speaking to the rector—I don't mean to-night. You will make no objection to coming soon to Hartledon?"

"I can't come, you know, as long as Lady Kirton is its mistress," she said, half seriously, half jestingly.

He laughed at the notion. Lady Kirton must be going soon of her own accord; if not, he should have to pluck up courage and give her a hint, was his answer. At any rate, she'd surely take herself off before Christmas. The old Dowager at Hartledon after he had Anne there! Not if he knew it, he added, as he went on with her into the presence of Dr. and Mrs. Ashton. The rector started from his seat, at once telling him that he ought not to have come in. Which the earl did not see at all, and decidedly refused to go out again.

Meanwhile the Countess Dowager and Maude were wondering what had become of him. They supposed he was still sitting in the dining-room. The old Dowager fidgeted about, her fingers ominously near the bell. She was burning to send to him, but hardly knew how he might take the message: it might be that the earl would object to go into leading-strings, and her attempt to put them on would ruin all. But the time went on; grew late; and she was dying for her tea, which she had chosen should wait for the earl also. Maude sat before the fire in a large chair; her eyes, her hands, her whole air utterly still, supremely listless.

"Don't you want your tea, Maude?" suddenly cried her mother, who had cast innumerable glances at her from time to time.

"I have wanted it hours and hours—as it seems to me."

"It's a horrid custom for young men, the sitting long after dinner. If he gets into it—But you must see to that, Maude, and stop it; if ever you reign at Hartledon. I daresay he's smoking."

"If ever I do reign at Hartledon—which I am not likely to do—I'll take care not to wait tea for any one, as you have made me wait for it this evening," was Lady Maude's rejoinder, spoken with apathy.

"I'll send a message to him," decided Lady Kirton, ringing rather fiercely at the bell, which brought up a servant.

"Tell Lord Hartledon we are waiting tea for him."

"Lord Hartledon's not in, my lady."

"Not in!"

"He went out directly after dinner, as soon as he had drank his coffee."

"O," said the Countess Dowager. And she began to make the tea with a fierce vehemence— for it did not please her to have it brought in made—and broke one of the costly cups.

END OF VOL. I.

LONDON:
ROBSON AND SON, GREAT NORTHERN PRINTING WORKS,
PANCRAS ROAD, N.W.

Check Out More Titles From HardPress Classics Series In this collection we are offering thousands of classic and hard to find books. This series spans a vast array of subjects – so you are bound to find something of interest to enjoy reading and learning about.

Subjects:
Architecture
Art
Biography & Autobiography
Body, Mind &Spirit
Children & Young Adult
Dramas
Education
Fiction
History
Language Arts & Disciplines
Law
Literary Collections
Music
Poetry
Psychology
Science
…and many more.

Visit us at www.hardpress.net

Im The Story
personalised classic books

"Beautiful gift.. lovely finish. My Niece loves it, so precious!"

Helen R Brumfieldon

⭐⭐⭐⭐⭐

UNIQUE GIFT

FOR KIDS, PARTNERS AND FRIENDS

Timeless books such as:

 Kids

Alice in Wonderland · The Jungle Book · The Wonderful Wizard of Oz
Peter and Wendy · Robin Hood · The Prince and The Pauper
The Railway Children · Treasure Island · A Christmas Carol

 Adults

Romeo and Juliet · Dracula

Highly Customizable | **Change** Books Title | **Replace** Characters Names with yours | **Upload** Photos for inside page | **Add** Inscriptions

Visit
Im The Story .com
and order yours today!

CPSIA information can be obtained
at www.ICGtesting.com
Printed in the USA
BVHW081825120819
555665BV00016B/1686/P